Family Walks and Hikes in the Canadian Rockies

Volume 2

Family Walks and Hikes in the Canadian Rockies

Volume 2
Bragg Creek, Kananaskis,
Bow Valley, Banff, Moraine Lake,
Yoho, Icefields Parkway, Jasper

ANDREW NUGARA

RMB

For information on purchasing bulk quantities of this book, or to obtain media excerpts or invite the author to speak at an event, please visit rmbooks.com and select the "Contact" tab.

RMB | Rocky Mountain Books Ltd.
rmbooks.com
@rmbooks
facebook.com/rmbooks

Cataloguing data available from Library and Archives Canada
ISBN 9781771603058 (paperback)
ISBN 9781771603065 (electronic)

All photographs are by Andrew Nugara unless otherwise noted.
Cover photo by Marko Stavric

Printed and bound in Canada

We would like to also take this opportunity to acknowledge the traditional territories upon which we live and work. In Calgary, Alberta, we acknowledge the Niitsitapi (Blackfoot) and the people of the Treaty 7 region in Southern Alberta, which includes the Siksika, the Piikuni, the Kainai, the Tsuut'ina and the Stoney Nakoda First Nations, including Chiniki, Bearpaw, and Wesley First Nations. The City of Calgary is also home to Métis Nation of Alberta, Region III. In Victoria, British Columbia, we acknowledge the traditional territories of the Lkwungen (Esquimalt, and Songhees), Malahat, Pacheedaht, Scia'new, T'Sou-ke and W̱SÁNEĆ(Pauquachin, Tsartlip, Tsawout, Tseycum) peoples.

We acknowledge the financial support of the Government of Canada through the Canada Book Fund and the Canada Council for the Arts, and of the province of British Columbia through the British Columbia Arts Council and the Book Publishing Tax Credit.

Disclaimer

The actions described in this book may be considered inherently dangerous activities. Individuals undertake these activities at their own risk. The information put forth in this guide has been collected from a variety of sources and is not guaranteed to be completely accurate or reliable. Many conditions and some information may change owing to weather and numerous other factors beyond the control of the authors and publishers. Individuals or groups must determine the risks, use their own judgment, and take full responsibility for their actions. Do not depend on any information found in this book for your own personal safety. Your safety depends on your own good judgment based on your skills, education, and experience.

It is up to the users of this guidebook to acquire the necessary skills for safe experiences and to exercise caution in potentially hazardous areas. The authors and publishers of this guide accept no responsibility for your actions or the results that occur from another's actions, choices, or judgments. If you have any doubt as to your safety or your ability to attempt anything described in this guidebook, do not attempt it.

CONTENTS

INTRODUCTION

About Family Walks and Hikes

Personally, I cannot think of many better ways to bond as a family than to hike as a family. The physical, mental and emotional benefits of hiking are undeniable, and who better to share and reap those benefits with than the ones you love and cherish the most?

Families living near the Canadian Rockies are fortunate to be close to some of the best hiking routes the planet has to offer. This book describes some of the more popular trips in these mountains that are appropriate for kids of all ages, adding to the trips offered in *Family Walks and Hikes in the Canadian Rockies Volume 1*. So grab the kids, get in the car and enjoy!

The challenges of family hiking

Hiking with young people poses unique challenges. How do you pick the most appropriate trails for your family (see "How the trails were chosen," below)? How do you balance long driving times with fidgety bodies? And how do you keep kids motivated and moving once you are on the trail? The following are some tips that will help make your family hiking experience more enjoyable:

- Candy: While hiking, a treat every 10 to 15 minutes can provide the motivation kids need to keep moving.
- Bikes and Striders: Bring them whenever possible. Kids love to bike – it's no secret!
- Hiking Games: Learn some hiking games for kids. Examples include I spy; scavenger hunts; follow the leader (with everyone taking turns as leader); red light, green light; I'm going on a picnic and other alphabet games; 20 questions; songs; and so on.
- Other Families: Hike with another or multiple families. In general, kids love to hike with other kids.
- Water: The connection humans (especially kids) have with water is undeniable. Any trip that involves water (lakes, rivers, waterfalls, creeks, beaver ponds) is likely to be a hit with the young ones.

- Environmental Awareness: Whenever possible, educate your kids about the local environment and wildlife, and the benefits and responsibilities of hiking in the mountains (but don't beat them over the head with it).
- Bribes: A little bribery goes a long way. If kids know there is an ice cream run at the end of the hike, they are more likely to be motivated to keep going.
- Know Your Limits: Know when to push kids and when it's time to give in. You can always try again another day.
- Backup: Have a backup plan – another hike or a different activity.
- Be patient, be patient, and then be patient.

Getting there
See the area maps on pages xvii and xviii. Trips in this book encompass a large area, starting at the south end of Highway 40 and reaching as far north as Jasper. All trips must be accessed by car.

Seasonal road closures
Road closures are unlikely to affect family hiking, as the restrictions occur in winter and spring. However, the closures are outlined below for those adventurous families that might want to hike in seasons other than summer.
- Highway 40 from December 1 to June 15, between Kananaskis Trail and Highwood Junction.
- Highway 66 from December 1 to May 15, west of Elbow Falls.
- Moraine Lake Road from mid-October to mid-May (may vary).
- Yoho Valley Road (Takakkaw Falls area) from October to mid-June.
- Cavell Road from October 15 to June 14 (may vary).

Facilities
Banff, Bragg Creek, Calgary, Canmore, Cochrane, Field (for Yoho National Park), Lake Louise (for Moraine Lake) and Jasper have all the amenities.

- Highway 1A (Exshaw): Heart Mountain Store (cafe, groceries, gas).
- Highway 1X (Bow Valley Provincial Park): small store at Bow Valley Campground.
- Highway 1 (Dead Man's Flats): gas, motel, small grocery store.
- Highway 40 (Kananaskis): many facilities, including an outdoor rental store in Kananaskis Village, a restaurant at Boundary Ranch and a gas station at Fortress Junction.
- Highway 93 North (Icefields Parkway): gas, restaurant, small store at the Saskatchewan River Crossing.

Weather

The best family hiking months in the Canadian Rockies are generally July, August and September. The temperature can reach the mid-30s in July and August, but it cools down quite a bit in September. Afternoon thunderstorms sometimes form during the hot months. Of course, snow can be expected in any month of the year but usually stays away in July and most of August. The different areas described in this book have slightly dissimilar hiking seasons and weather patterns:

- Bragg Creek is generally snow-free by April, but some areas are not accessible until May 15 because of the road closure. The hiking season goes well into October and even November.
- The hiking season at the north end of Highway 40 lasts from May to October. This area is often the best place to hike when the weather farther west is not ideal.
- At the south end of Highway 40, especially in the Highwood area and Kananaskis Lakes, snow can sometimes linger into July. September is often great for hiking here, with long periods of stable weather.
- Banff experiences a July–September family hiking season that sometimes extends into October.
- Moraine Lake and Highway 93 North can have snow lingering well into July. An early-season snow will usually

end the hiking season in early October. Routes in these areas are also prone to be cloudier than other places due to their location on or near the Continental Divide.

- Hiking in and around Jasper can be feasible by June, but in some years snow will linger well into July. In general the hiking season comes to a close in October.

What to wear

Hiking boots, as opposed to runners, are recommended for adults on most of the trails. However, appropriate gear may differ for young children. They are generally less susceptible to the types of ankle injuries that adults might sustain. And of course, children outgrow their footwear annually (sometimes monthly). A sturdy pair of runners with good tread will suffice for most of the routes described here. Kids who are up for more advanced trips, such as King Creek Ridge and the Windtower, will need hiking boots with good ankle support. Bring a rain jacket and warm clothes, as the weather can change dramatically and very quickly. For those hot summer days, bring sunscreen, a hat and bug repellent.

Drinking water

To be safe, it is best to bring potable water from your home, hotel or campsite. Natural sources may be contaminated with *Giardia lamblia*, a parasite that can cause severe gastrointestinal problems. At higher elevations, it is generally safe to drink from streams without treating the water. Filtering water is also an option.

Wildlife concerns

Wildlife is abundant in every area described in this book. As exciting as it is for kids to see animals in their natural habitats, it is important that all hikers try to avoid wildlife encounters. Bears, moose, deer, elk, bighorn sheep and marmots are the most common types of wildlife you might encounter, but wolves, cougars and coyotes could also present themselves. When hiking, make lots of noise to warn bears and other wildlife that you are there. Moose and elk can be aggressive in the fall, during mating season – steer well clear if you encounter them.

Of course, feeding wildlife is a strict no-no. Please discourage this tempting but very harmful behaviour.

Another form of wildlife prevalent throughout the Canadian Rockies is the tick. From March to the end of June, ticks ravenously feed on any mammal they can sink their hooks into, humans included. Check yourself and your kids very carefully after any early season hike. DEET products (for your skin) and permethrin products (for your clothes) can be used to ward off these disease-ridden creatures.

Safety tips

A few pointers to help ensure your family experience is a safe and fulfilling one:

- Hike together, especially when your kids are younger.
- Don't be lulled into a false sense of security because you are in a larger group. You still must make noise to warn bears and other wildlife of your presence.
- Carry bear spray and know how to use it.
- Consider using a personal locator device, such as SPOT, in case of an emergency.
- Stay on designated trails unless you are experienced and/or familiar with the challenges of off-trail hiking/scrambling.
- Check the weather forecast before setting out. Also, check online resources and the designated park's visitor centre for trail conditions and trail and area closures.
- Afternoon thunderstorms are common in the summer. Start early to avoid them.

Campgrounds

Camping with kids can be a blast, a nightmare and everything in between. It is best to inundate them with camping experiences at a young age, so they get a feel for it and learn to love it.

Many campgrounds give easy access to the hikes described in this book. A few are listed here, but check the internet for a complete listing. For example, the Bragg Creek & Kananaskis Outdoor Recreation website (bckor.ca) lists all the campgrounds in the Bragg Creek area, as well as many campgrounds in other areas such as Canmore, Highway 40 and Highwood. Some campgrounds allow you to book online, but others operate on a first-come, first-served basis.

- Elbow Valley: Beaver Flats, Paddy's Flat, Little Elbow. Call 403.949.3132.
- Highway 40 north end and Bow Valley: Bow Valley Provincial Park. Call 1.877.537.2757 or reserve online.
- Highway 40 south end and Kananaskis Trail: Elbow Lake (backcountry). Call 403.678.0760 or book online. For Boulton Creek, Canyon, Elkwood, Interlakes and Lower Lake, call 403.591.7226.
- Banff, Kootenay, Lake Louise: Tunnel Mountain Village, Two Jack Lake, Johnston Canyon and Lake Louise. Book online for all.
- Highway 93 North: Mosquito Creek, Silverhorn Creek, Waterfowl Lakes, Rampart Creek (reserve online), Wilcox, Icefield, Jonas, Honeymoon Lake, Kerkeslin, Wabasso (reserve online). Unless otherwise noted, all are first-come, first served.
- Jasper: Snaring, Wapiti (reserve online), Whistler (family-oriented).

Using this Book

How the trails were chosen

Choosing routes for family hiking is fraught with challenges. Driving time, trip length, elevation gain and quality of the trail are but a few of the many factors you must consider and scrutinize when attempting to determine if a route is a good candidate for a family hike. Add to that the wide range of fitness levels and abilities of children and accompanying adults, and you end up with a process that is far from an exact science.

The routes in this book are mostly short, already-popular hiking trails. Preference has been given to routes that are varied and have multiple points of interest, which hopefully will keep kids (and adults) engaged and motivated. As much as possible, routes with options to extend the length of the trip have been chosen, so you can play it by ear and change the objective as you go. This also accommodates "advanced" family hikers who are used to longer and more strenuous trips. For example, if the objective is Larch Valley and the kids have no issues making it that far, you could extend the trip to include Sentinel Pass.

In picking a specific trip for your family, the adults in charge usually know best. You might have a 5-year-old who can hike every trail in this book without breaking a sweat or batting an eyelid. Conversely, your 10-year-old might struggle with even the easiest of trails. It is up to you to choose trips that best fit your family's abilities. On that note, it is always best to err on the side of caution and be conservative in choosing. As much as possible, I have tried to include short and longer hikes within short driving distances of one another, giving families the option to complete multiple hikes in one day if one hike is not enough. For example, after hiking Nihahi Ridge, you could stop at Forgetmenot Pond for a relaxing rest/picnic and a very short hike; or if you arrive at Moraine Lake and determine that the Larch Valley hike may be too much for your crew, the Moraine Lake shoreline hike is right there.

Trails

Parks Canada, Alberta Parks and other organizations have done an outstanding job of creating and maintaining the trails described in this book. Most of these trails are well marked and well signed. Therefore, many of the route descriptions in this book are brief, requiring very little detail. Even the routes without any signage are generally easy to follow.

Optional add-ons to extend your trip

Some trips in this book include optional add-ons: trips you can tack on to the main hike if you have the time and energy. Look for these **Going Farther** sections if your family usually has the stamina to combine adventures.

Location

This section provides the driving instructions you will need to get to the start of each trip, from Calgary.

Distance

Distances represent the round-trip distance for each trip.

Elevation gain

Elevation gain represents the total height gained for each round trip, including any significant ups and downs along the way.

Difficulty and age recommendations

Levels of difficulty in this book describe conditions underfoot and the steepness of trail grades. The difficulty rating assumes good hiking conditions, so bear in mind that adverse weather or snowy conditions may elevate the rating.

The age recommendations in the difficulty ratings should be considered general guidelines. Knowing your children's abilities and limitations is key. The recommendations assume children will be able to complete the entire trip on their own two feet. If you are carrying kids in baby carriers, the recommendations do not apply.

Season

Season describes the suggested times of the year to go on each hike. However, weather (specifically snow) can affect those suggestions quite dramatically. Areas farther west are especially prone to early snowfall that can render many routes off limits or at least unwise to travel on. Conversely, there are other parts of the Rockies, such as the Elbow Valley, that may be snow-free as early as May and well into October.

Of special interest for children

Included in this section of a trip description are recommendations for combining trips, Chariot- (jogging stroller-) friendly trips, preferable time of year to undertake the route and other tidbits that may make the trip more enjoyable for the kids (and you).

Sketch maps

Red lines indicate main trails. Dashed red lines indicate optional routes and/or trip extension routes.

Do I need any other maps?

The maps provided for each trip provide all the information needed to perform the hike; there should be no need to carry other maps. However, for those who like to carry a complete map, NTS (National Topographic System) and Gem Trek produce excellent maps for all areas covered by this book. MEC, Atmosphere and many bookstores carry these maps.

If you would prefer a digital map, download the Topo Maps Canada app on your phone. The app uses a satellite signal, not a cell-phone signal, to pinpoint your exact location and then shows that location on a topographical map. Even if you are far out of cell-signal range, the app can still determine your location. The maps on Topo Maps Canada also show many of the trails in this book.

Doing More

If at some point in your family hiking journey you realize the family is ready for more challenging trips than the ones described in this book, pick up any or all of the following:

- the five volumes of *Gillean Daffern's Kananaskis Country Trail Guide*;
- other volumes in the *Popular Day Hikes* series;
- *Canadian Rockies Trail Guide*, by Brian Patton and Bart Robinson;
- *Classic Hikes in the Canadian Rockies*, by Graeme Pole;
- *Canadian Rockies Access Guide*, by John Dodd and Gail Helgason; and
- *Where Locals Hike in the Canadian Rockies*, by Kathy and Craig Copeland.

For those families who want to experience the Rockies year-round, consider cross-country skiing and snowshoeing trips. *Ski Trails in the Canadian Rockies*, 5th Edition, by Chic Scott and

Darren Farley, and *A Beginner's Guide to Snowshoeing in the Canadian Rockies*, 2nd Edition, by Andrew Nugara, are great places to start.

The logical extension of hiking is scrambling – getting to the top of a mountain without technical means (i.e., ropes and climbing equipment). Generally this activity is for adults, but older children who show specific aptitude for advanced hiking may be up for it. For detailed information and route descriptions, acquire copies of Alan Kane's *Scrambles in the Canadian Rockies*, 3rd Edition, and *More Scrambles in the Canadian Rockies*, 3rd Edition, by Andrew Nugara.

AREA MAP, TRIPS 1–20

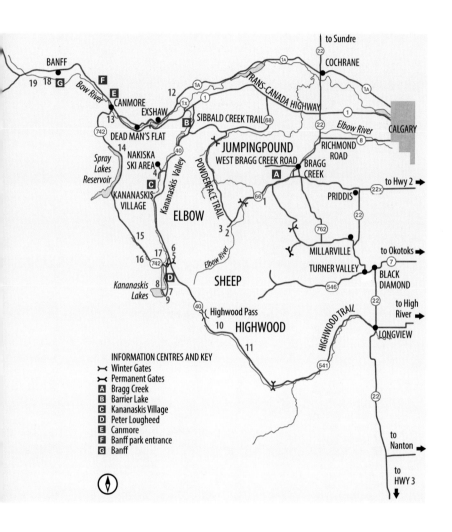

INFORMATION CENTRES AND KEY
- Winter Gates
- Permanent Gates
- **A** Bragg Creek
- **B** Barrier Lake
- **C** Kananaskis Village
- **D** Peter Lougheed
- **E** Canmore
- **F** Banff park entrance
- **G** Banff

AREA MAP, TRIPS 21–47

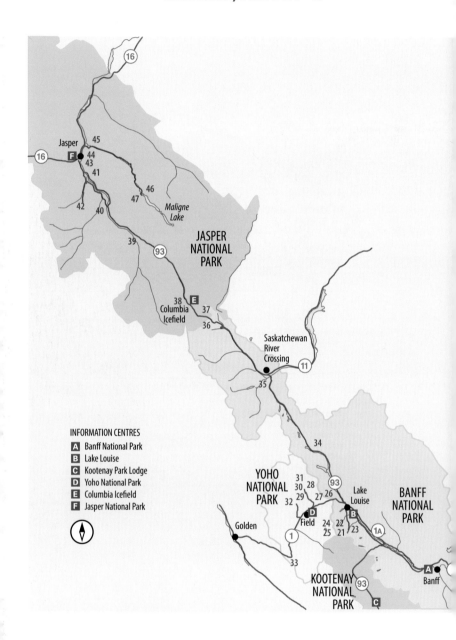

INFORMATION CENTRES

A Banff National Park
B Lake Louise
C Kootenay Park Lodge
D Yoho National Park
E Columbia Icefield
F Jasper National Park

Highway 66, the Elbow

HIGHWAY 66, THE ELBOW

The Elbow (so named because of the Elbow River) is the closest mountain area to Calgary and therefore driving time is minimal. For the average "Are we there yet?" child, this is a good thing! The trails are excellent and generally easy to follow, with minimal elevation gain, and have enough points of interest to keep kids engaged. Hiking in the Elbow Valley is ideal for younger children, but the older ones will undoubtedly enjoy it too.

The area has undergone recent upgrades to improve the overall hiking experience. Many of the most popular hikes are described in Volume 1 of *Family Walks and Hikes*; however, three have been added to this volume. Hiking up Nihahi Ridge with the family and then relaxing at Forgetmenot Pond makes for a terrific day out.

The quaint hamlet of Bragg Creek offers all amenities and facilities for a stop on the drive in or out.

PREVIOUS PAGE Fun at Paddy's Flat. Kian Nugara jumps the waterway.

1. PADDY'S FLAT INTERPRETIVE TRAIL

A very pleasant loop of forest and river hiking,
with some great play spots for the kids.

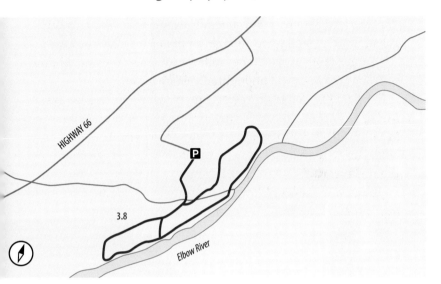

LOCATION
Drive west on Highway 1, south on Highway 22 and turn left at the four-way stop in Bragg Creek. Turn right onto Highway 66, drive 13.1 km and turn left into the Paddy's Flat campground. Stay right and then turn left into the B, C loop. Go down a hill and park opposite a playground.

DISTANCE
3.8-km loop

ELEVATION GAIN
46 m

DIFFICULTY
Moderate, recommended for children aged 3 and older. Good trail all the way, but there are many intersecting trails that may cause confusion. Look at the trail map carefully and follow your nose!

CLOCKWISE FROM TOP LEFT Always a good idea to discuss the trail map with the kids; Lindsay, Nicole a dogs Copper and Mary hike through pleasant forest before reaching the river; The first area you re by the river is fantastic for some kid fun, as the Nugara clan demonstrates

SEASON

Late spring, summer and early fall.

OF SPECIAL INTEREST FOR CHILDREN

Kids will love the rocky and sandy areas by the river. There are places where the kids can get their feet wet, but choose carefully and keep an eye on them – the river is deep and fast flowing in places.

1. The signed trail starts at the right side of the parking lot. Take a good look at the trail map. Follow the trail to a T-junction and turn right.

2. Follow this trail as it parallels the Elbow River but some distance away from it and above it. Ignore a trail that veers off to the left, heading down to the river.

3. The trail ends up near the campground road and then takes a sharp left turn, going downhill. Follow it to the Riverview junction. The recommended route here is to turn right onto the Riverview trail and follow it until you see a minor trail at the left that goes down to the river.

4. Take the trail down to the bank of the Elbow River and hike downstream. There are many beautiful places here for the kids to play and explore the area. Several sandy areas are quite beach-like.

5. Continue going downstream, sometimes right along the river and sometimes on the trail that parallels the river. Another scenic, beachy area is soon reached. If you want to call it a day here, it is possible at this point to ascend a trail back to the main trail you started on and then return to the parking lot.

6. The recommended route is to keep following the trail downstream. The trail eventually turns away from the river and then basically U-turns and heads back to the parking lot through pleasant forest.

2. FORGETMENOT POND

Short and easy with great views. Quiet and peaceful in the morning and a wild party in the afternoon on a hot summer day! More of a rest stop and play area than a hike, but well worth it.

LOCATION
Drive west on Highway 1, south on Highway 22 and turn left at the four-way stop in Bragg Creek. From the intersection of Highway 22 and Highway 66 turn right and drive 28 km west on Highway 66. Turn left into Little Elbow and follow the signs to the Forgetmenot parking lot.

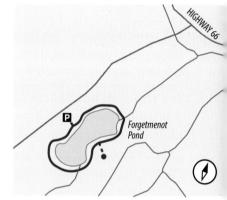

DISTANCE
1-km loop

ELEVATION GAIN
None

DIFFICULTY
Very easy, recommended for all; excellent paved trail around the pond.

SEASON
Late spring, summer and fall.

OF SPECIAL INTEREST FOR CHILDREN
Bring a raft, canoe or other flotation device if you want to get in the water. Fishing is allowed and the path is stroller-friendly.

1.   Hike the trail in either direction around the pond.

2.   Optional: For some extra exercise and views, the Elbow River is close by and easy to explore.

M TOP Peaceful, serene Forgetmenot Pond on a clear calm morning; Natalie Kindt, Russell Doll, Kindt and Dawson Kindt appear to be enjoying their time at the pond (Courtesy Melissa Kindt)

3. NIHAHI RIDGE

A very popular trip with the option to
reach a significant summit.

LOCATION
Drive west on Highway 1, south on Highway 22 and turn left at the four-way stop in Bragg Creek. From the intersection of Highway 22 and Highway 66, turn right and drive 28 km west on Highway 66. Turn left into Little Elbow and follow the signs to the trailhead parking.

DISTANCE
5.6 km return

ELEVATION GAIN
365 m; high point: 1981 m

DIFFICULTY
Strenuous, recommended for children aged 7 and older. Good trail for most of the trip, with some rocky terrain.

South Summit
0.8
South Viewpoint
0.8
End of Official Trail
1.2
Little Elbow River
Glasgow Creek
Ford Creek
1.6

SEASON
Late spring, summer and fall.

OF SPECIAL INTEREST FOR CHILDREN
The first 1.6 km from the parking lot to the trail is easily bikeable and fun on the return. The Going Farther is a great introduction to advanced hiking and scrambling.

1. From the end of the parking lot, hike or bike the Little Elbow trail (orange signs), eventually ascending to the campground road.

ah Koob arrives at the beautiful open meadow that precedes the hike to the south end of the
ge (Courtesy Tanya Koob).

2. Hike past the campground to the official start of the trail (kiosk and map).

3. Keep going for about 500 m and look to the right for the Little Elbow trail sign and map (about 1.6 km from the parking lot). Leave the bikes here if you rode. Turn right onto this trail.

4. Follow the trail through forest, veering left at one point and then turning right at the Nihahi Ridge Trail sign.

5. The trail goes up through a beautiful open meadow, and then up to the south end of the ridge.

6. Turn right and follow the ridge up, enjoying improving views in all directions.

7. There is no official end to Nihahi Ridge Trail. Simply follow the ridge until you arrive at an open rocky plateau with orangish-coloured rock. This occurs right after a very short but noticeably steep step in the ridge. Enjoy the view and then return the same way you came in, or continue on to the south viewpoint and/or the south end of Nihahi Ridge.

Once you are on the ridge, the route is obvious. The trail ends (unsigned) a few hundred metres before the steep rock band.

Going Farther: South Viewpoint

For advanced family hikers looking for an even better view and who are comfortable on loose, steep terrain.

Distance
Add 1.6 km return

Elevation Gain
Add 250 m; high point: 2231 m

Difficulty
Very strenuous, recommended for children aged 10 and older. Steep, rocky terrain and some minor scrambling.

1. Continue following the trail up the ridge towards the significant rock band.

2. Approaching the rock band the trail veers to the right and traverses below the ridge before heading steeply up to the ridge.

3. Continue following the good trail, again on the right side of the ridge. The crux is eventually reached – a short step up a diagonal crack (see photo). Hand- and footholds are plentiful, but check with the kids to make sure they will be able to get down.

FROM LEFT Approaching the crux rock band. The route goes up the weakness near the left side of the photo; From the South Viewpoint, looking up to the south summit of Nihahi Ridge.

4. Above the crux, hike a very short distance south to a cairn and an excellent viewpoint. This is not the summit, but many will want to call it a day here and return the same way they came in.

Going Farther: South Summit
The icing on the cake for young scramblers.

Distance
Add 1.6 km return

Elevation Gain
Add 155 m; high point: 2386 m

Difficulty
Very strenuous, recommended for children aged 12 and older. Steep, rocky terrain and some minor scrambling.

1. The trail continues up the mountain. Near the top (crux), look for yellow paint marks on the rock. The easiest place to ascend this final rock step is farther left of the paint. Above the crux it's a short hike to the south end. Note that this is not the south summit of Nihahi Ridge. Getting to that summit is a moderate scramble and will feel very exposed and precarious to many – not a place for kids. Return the same way you came in.

COUNTER-CLOCKWISE FROM TOP Nihahi Ridge, page 8. The upper part of the mountain looks deceivingly steep, but its bark is far worse than its bite; Someone is practising for those future knife edged ridges! Noah and Mark Koob complete the ascent (Courtesy Tanya Koob); The crux of the upper section. Mr. Koob leads his son Noah up the steep rock. For younger kids, a rope is a good id (Courtesy Tanya Koob).

Highway 40 South,
Kananaskis Trail

HIGHWAY 40 SOUTH, KANANASKIS TRAIL

Driving time from the Calgary city limits to the north end of Highway 40 is only about 30 minutes, but expect to take 45–60 minutes to get to any trailhead. Hikes along the Kananaskis Trail and in the Highwood area (Arethusa Cirque and Picklejar Lakes) require approximately 1.75–2 hours of driving time.

Though somewhat of a longer drive, Arethusa Cirque is highly recommended for the younger ones. King Creek Ridge will be a real feather in one's cap for older kids.

Facilities and amenities along Highway 40 are fairly limited. However, a stop for ice cream or treats in Kananaskis Village (about 26 km south on Highway 40) can be a good motivating factor for kids. There is also a playground in the village. Fortress Junction has a gas station and ice cream.

PREVIOUS PAGE Amélie and Aven Stavric at Upper Kananaskis Lake (Courtesy Marko Stavric).

4. COAL MINE

Mostly a pleasant forest hike, but with a wonderful open view at the end and the option to hike some of Centennial Ridge.

LOCATION
Drive west on Highway 1, then south on Highway 40 (Exit 118) for 23 km and turn right, towards Kananaskis Village. Drive 600 m and turn left, then turn right, into the Ribbon Creek parking lot.

DISTANCE
4.6 km return

ELEVATION GAIN
246 m

DIFFICULTY
Moderate, recommended for children aged 5 and older. Good, well-signed trail throughout.

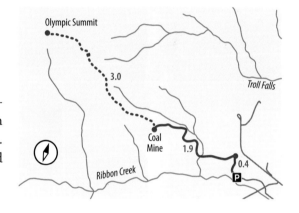

SEASON
Summer and fall.

OF SPECIAL INTEREST FOR CHILDREN
Mid-July is great for wildflowers, late September for larches (Centennial Ridge only).

1. The signed trailhead is near the northwest end of the parking lot. Hike the Hidden Trail for 400 m to a four-way signed junction. Turn left.

2. Hike another 500 m to another signed junction. Stay on the main trail. The left fork is the Centennial Ridge Trail and is a good option for the descent.

3. The next 1.5 km is very straightforward. Simply stay on the main trail, ignoring the intersections with the Centennial Ridge Trail. Near the end, the trail narrows and then magically

COUNTER-CLOCKWISE FROM TOP Emi, Miya and Karen Ung arrive at the clearing near the end of the hike (Courtesy Kheang Ung; playoutsideguide.com); Mike Miller steps out into the beautifully open terrain. Fall colours can be very rewarding; Rob Miller, Mike Miller and Nicole Lisafeld descend open terrain below the Mine Scar. The ridge above is part of Centennial Ridge.

emerges from the forest onto an open hillside, granting terrific views of the valley below (high wow factor here!). Continue on the narrow trail until it abruptly ends in the middle of the hillside meadow.

4. Return the same way you came in, or go a little (or a lot) farther, as described below. On the descent, you can shave off

about 400 m of hiking by using the Centennial Ridge Trail. This trail has been realigned and is not as steep as it used to be.

5. Optional and Recommended: Above the meadow sits what is now commonly referred to as the "Mine Scar" – an open face of rock where mining once occurred. It's an easy hike up to the rock and then to a small plateau. Here you will find the Centennial Ridge Trail right above you. Return the same way you came in or, for a little variety, descend the Centennial Ridge Trail.

Going Farther: Centennial Ridge
One of the premier steep hikes in Kananaskis Country – for experienced families only. Gain 100 m for an improved view of the valley, go all the way to Olympic Summit 700 vertical metres above, or anything in between.

Distance
Add 1–6 km return

Elevation Gain
100–700 m

Difficulty
Moderate to very strenuous, recommended for children aged 12 and older. Good but consistently steep trail throughout.

1. From the end of the Coal Mine trail, hike up to the small plateau, as described above, and then up a small hill to the Centennial Ridge Trail sign.

2. Follow the steep trail up through the trees, eventually arriving at another open area that offers the second stellar view of the day.

3. From this point on, it is up to you how far you go. The trail is superb all the way but relentlessly steep. The ultimate goal would be the summit of Mount Allan (one of the most

rewarding ascents in the Kananaskis). However, this involves almost 1400 m of elevation gain and takes about 8–10 hours round trip – wait until the kids are old enough to vote! A more realistic, but still rewarding and very physically strenuous, objective is Olympic Summit, about 600 vertical metres above.

4. Continue grinding your way up the steep trail. The route is obvious. The only obstacle is a significant rock band that appears to bar the way. Follow the trail around the right side of the rock band for a short distance until the route cuts steeply up to the left. A few scrambling moves are required, but nothing too strenuous or scary. Be sure, however, that everyone is going to be comfortable coming down this way.

5. Above the rock band, hike another few hundred metres to the several obvious cairned summits (collectively, they are often referred to as "Olympic Summit"). It is worth visiting all the high points. Enjoy a magnificent summit panorama and then return the same way you came in. Although the summit of Mount Allan looks relatively close, this is an illusion – it is a good 1.5 hours and 400 m of elevation gain away.

...ING PAGE It's only a steep ten-minute hike ...m the top of the Coal Mine trail to this ...nderful viewpoint (Courtesy HikeBikeTravel. ...m). **THIS PAGE, TOP TO BOTTOM** Three hikers ...se in on the crux rock band. The route goes ...und the right side (Courtesy HikeBikeTravel. ...m); A very small sample of the wildflowers ...t litter the slopes by mid-July and some ...he ever-improving views; The reward ...naking the westernmost high point of ...mpic Summit is this amazing view of Mount ...n (right) and Wind Mountain (left) (Courtesy ...eBikeTravel.com).

5. KING CREEK RIDGE

One of the most strenuous and steep trips in the book, but so worth the effort.

LOCATION
Drive west on Highway 1, then south on Highway 40 (Exit 118) for 49 km to the King Creek day use parking lot on the left side of the road.

DISTANCE
7 km return

ELEVATION GAIN
720 m; high point: 2423 m

DIFFICULTY
Very strenuous, recommended for children aged 12 and older. Good trail throughout, but relentlessly steep up to the ridge.

SEASON
Summer and early fall.

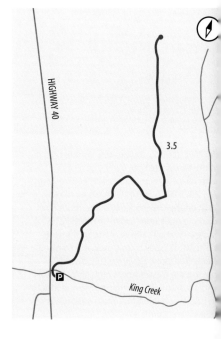

OF SPECIAL INTEREST FOR CHILDREN
Fantastic ridge walk and spectacular summit views. Similar to Little Lawson but much steeper. One of the most advanced trips in the book.

1. From the parking lot, walk back towards Highway 40. Just before reaching the highway, turn right onto an obvious trail that traverses the embankment to the north side of King Creek.

CKWISE FROM TOP LEFT Stella Rosa Knight and Noah Koob ascend the trail where it's relatively gentle.
ets much steeper (Courtesy Tanya Koob); Noah and Stella enjoying the magnificent view of the
al Range to the east (Courtesy Tanya Koob); Adam and Yasmine Altubor, Stella Rosa Knight and
ah Koob taking in one of the many spectacular views from the ridge (Courtesy Tanya Koob).

2. The trail then turns east, ascends into the forest, drops down a little, goes up a short distance and veers left, traversing the hillside and going up slightly.

3. After about 5 minutes of traversing, the trail turns sharply right and starts the relentless uphill grind to the ridge, going in a generally easterly direction. There is some convolution of a number of different trails at a few points, but as long as you pick the most prominent one you should be good.

4. Upon reaching the ridge, turn left (north) and follow the trail for about 1.6 km to the first summit. Views improve quickly and reach the stunning level by the time you top out.

5. Optional: Traversing to the second, slightly higher summit about 200 m farther north is recommended, but step carefully near the summit. There is a terrific drop on the right side and a nasty little fall on the left if you slip.

6. Return the same way you came in. There is an alternate descent route down the steep east side and then down via King Creek, but it is not recommended for kids.

6. KING CREEK CANYON

A classic creek hike up a very interesting canyon.

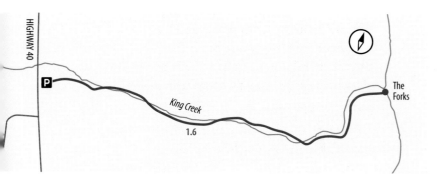

LOCATION
Drive west on Highway 1, then south on Highway 40 (Exit 118) for 49 km to the King Creek day use parking lot.

DISTANCE
3.2 km return

ELEVATION GAIN
120 m

DIFFICULTY
Moderate, recommended for children aged 5 and older. Short sections of trail, but mostly a rocky off-trail hike with numerous creek crossings, usually on logs or rocks but sometimes right in the water.

SEASON
Summer and early fall.

OF SPECIAL INTEREST FOR CHILDREN
The kids will love all the creek crossings on logs, and some will love just walking through the water. Note, however, that floods and/or high water levels can change the canyon throughout the season. Everyone should have footwear they don't mind getting wet.

1. A specific description is unnecessary. Hike up the canyon on both sides of the creek, sometimes using snippets of trails or walking along the side of the creek. More than likely everyone will have to ford the creek at several points where there are no logs or rocks. The crux is a narrowing of the creek where you have to scramble across a short section of rock on the left side of the creek.

2. Continue all the way to where the creek forks. Return the same way you came in.

FROM LEFT Skye, Kian and Rogan Nugara negotiate a tricky rocky section; The crux. Rogan is over and it's Kian's turn to tackle the tricky step.

7. CANADIAN MOUNT EVEREST EXPEDITION TRAIL

Another pleasant trail with many informative interpretive signs. Decent views from the high point, but much of it is blocked by trees.

LOCATION
Drive west on Highway 1, then south on Highway 40 (Exit 118) for 49 km to the Kananaskis Lakes turn-off. Turn right and follow the road for 12.7 km, and turn left into the Canadian Mount Everest Expedition parking lot.

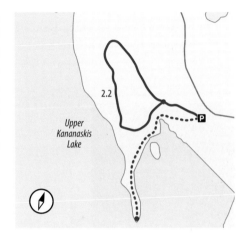

DISTANCE
2.2-km loop

ELEVATION GAIN
104 m; high point: 1813 m

DIFFICULTY
Moderately easy, recommended for children aged 4 and older. Good trail all the way, with some steep sections.

SEASON
Late spring, summer and fall.

OF SPECIAL INTEREST FOR CHILDREN
Take the time to stop and read the interpretive signs. The optional trip to the peninsula can be fun for kids when the water level is low.

1. The trail starts just to the right of the trailhead sign. It's easy to follow and no instructions are required. Be sure to do the trail as a loop by taking the right fork when the trail divides.

2. The view from the high point is limited because of trees. Better views are experienced a short ways down the other side.

3. Optional: For more open views of the lake, hike the trail that starts to the left of the trailhead sign. This trail follows the lakeshore, heading west and northwest. When the water level of the lake is low, it's possible to hike along a very cool rocky peninsula – fun for the kids. Go as far as you feel like and then return the same way. The continuation of this trail goes all the way to the North Interlakes parking lot (see next trip), if you don't mind an additional 8.6 km of good hiking!

FROM LEFT Most of the trail goes through forest and has several fun little obstacles for kids to negotiate. Kiran Boora makes easy work of the tree root section (Courtesy Par Boora); Many interesting interpretive panels at the high point.

8. UPPER KANANASKIS LAKE

A scenic hike around the north side of one of the Roc,
premier lakes (actually, it's now classified as a reservoir).

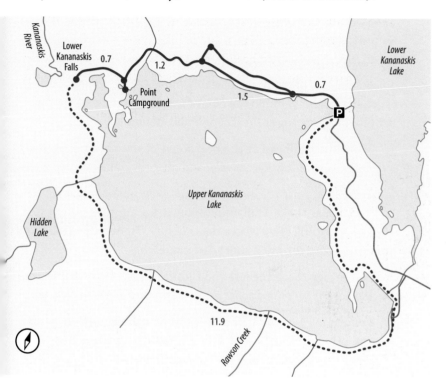

LOCATION
Drive west on Highway 1, then south on Highway 40 (Exit 118) for 49 km to the Kananaskis Lakes turnoff. Turn right and follow the road for 14.8 km, then turn left into the North Interlakes parking lot.

DISTANCE
7.2–8.4 km return

ELEVATION GAIN
50 m

DIFFICULTY

Moderate, recommended for children aged 6 and older. Hard-packed mud trail, followed by a rocky trail through a boulder field. There is optional off-trail travel on loose, rocky terrain.

SEASON

Summer and fall.

OF SPECIAL INTEREST FOR CHILDREN

Two kilometres of the trail is bikeable, but there are some rocky sections. Exploration around the Point Campground may be the highlight for kids; staying at the campground, doubly so.

1. From the trailhead at the north end of the parking lot, hike northwest alongside the lake and over the dam.

2. Turn left onto the unsigned but wide and obvious Upper Kananaskis Lake Trail, and follow it for another 600 m to a signed intersection where the trail forks (ignore the trail that veers off to the left a short distance along).

3. At the sign, both the left and right forks are feasible, but the left fork is recommended, as it offers good views of the lake.

4. Follow this trail for 1.5 km to another signed junction, where the other fork joins up. A few hundred metres before this junction the trail enters a boulder field. The trail is a little trickier to follow here but still pronounced.

5. At the signed junction, keep going in westerly and southwesterly directions for 1.2 km to a signed junction marking the Point Campground. It isn't necessary to go into the campground, but exploring the lakeshore around it could be the highlight of the day for the kids. Hike to the first campsite (being considerate of all campers), then turn left and make your way over to the lakeshore. Depending on the level of the water, there may be two small islands that can be accessed by crossing the water using a line of strategically placed rocks. After exploring this beautiful area, return to the campground and then back to the campground entrance.

M LEFT Amélie and Aven Stavric return from a lakeside stroll. (Courtesy Marko Stavric); There are ough open views of the lake to keep everyone entertained along the way (Courtesy Off the Beaten :h, with Chris & Connie; BIGDoer.com).

6. At this point your options are to end the trip and return the same way you came in, or continue to Lower Kananaskis Falls, about 700 m away.

7. If going to the falls (recommended), continue west on the trail, arriving at a signed junction ("Waterfall Viewpoint") in about ten minutes. Turn left and hike down to a bench, where you can admire the cascading water. Return the same way you came in.

Going Farther: Complete the Loop

The "full meal deal" circles the entire lake. Recommended only for older and more experienced kids who are used to hiking significant distances. Expect to take 4.5–6 hours to complete the loop.

Distance
16 km for the entire loop

Elevation Gain
Add 50 m

Difficulty

Very strenuous, recommended for children aged 12 and older. Good trail all the way.

1. From the lower falls, go back up to the junction and turn left onto the main trail, which goes to a bridge across the river.

2. Cross the bridge and away you go. The next 7 km, around the west and south sides of the lake, are long and often uninspiring – great exercise, though! You will pass the Rawson Lake turnoff and Sarrail Falls (this is inspiring) near the end of the 7-km trek and end up at the Upper Lake parking lot.

3. Approaching the Upper Lake parking lot, stay on the trail to the left of it.

4. Hike past a boat launch and then over the rocky dam, always staying close to the lakeshore.

5. At the end of the dam, continue on the trail as it curves around to the left, cuts through a short section of forest and then resumes travel, now going north along the east shore of the lake. You are now on the Interlakes Trail. Thankfully, the last 4 km are considerably more interesting than the preceding 6 or so. The tree stumps lining the shore will assuredly be points of interest for kids. Near the end of the trail, watch for a narrow section with a steep drop on the left side.

FROM LEFT There are some pleasant views from the south shore of the lake (Courtesy Off the Beaten Path, with Chris & Connie; BIGDoer.com); Connie Biggart hikes across the dam that joins the boat launch to the Interlakes Trail (Courtesy Off the Beaten Path, with Chris & Connie; BIGDoer.com).

9. INTERLAKES TRAIL

*A lesser-known, but very interesting,
hike along the east shore of the lake.*

LOCATION
Drive west on Highway 1, then south on Highway 40 (Exit 118) for 49 km to the Kananaskis Lakes turnoff. Turn right and follow the road for 14.8 km, then turn left into the North Interlakes parking lot. Note that this trip can also be completed in the opposite direction, starting from the Canadian Mount Everest Expedition parking lot.

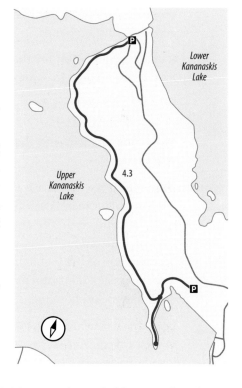

DISTANCE
8.6 km return or 4.3 km one-way with two vehicles

ELEVATION GAIN
50 m

DIFFICULTY
Moderate, recommended for children aged 4 and older. Good trail throughout, with options to hike along the shoreline. Watch for a narrow exposed section near the north end.

SEASON
Late spring, summer and fall.

OF SPECIAL INTEREST FOR CHILDREN
Swaths of huge tree stumps and shelters made from dead trees may be a source of interest for kids. When the water level is low, a small island near the north end is accessible. Early-morning trips on clear, calm days can grant amazing reflections in the lake.

1. The trail starts at the northwest end of the parking lot and heads in a southwest direction. It basically follows the shoreline for the 4.3 km of its length.

2. Early on, there is a narrow section of trail with a significant drop on the right side. Watch the little ones carefully here and/or hold their hands.

3. A small island is fun for the kids to explore when the water level is low enough to expose the land bridge to the island.

4. When possible, it's often preferable to leave the trail and travel on the rocky shore. One recommendation is to use the trail going one way and the lakeshore for the return trip or vice versa.

5. Near the south end, the trail approaches a fascinating rocky peninsula but veers away from it and curves around, eventually arriving near the trailhead for the Canadian Mount Everest Expedition. If the water level is low, this peninsula becomes one of the highlights of the trip for kids. Make your way there via a faint trail just after the main trail turns east, or via the rocky shoreline.

6. From the peninsula it's probably best to return generally the same way you came in, but following the shoreline if possible. It's not necessary to go to the Canadian Mount Everest Expedition trailhead unless you have a conveniently placed second vehicle there!

OM TOP Great views of the lakes only minutes away
>m the parking lot (Courtesy Off the Beaten Path, with
>ris & Connie; BIGDoer.com); Arriving at the peninsula
low water; From inside one of many tree shelters that
ve been constructed on the shore. Usually a big hit with
ds (Courtesy Off the Beaten Path, with Chris & Connie;
GDoer.com).

10. ARETHUSA CIRQUE

A lesser-known gem boasting some of the most impressive scenery in the Rockies, with options for a short hike or a more extensive loop route. A personal favourite.

LOCATION
Drive west on Highway 1, then south on Highway 40 (Exit 118) for approximately 67 km. Drive 1.4 km past the Ptarmigan Cirque/ Highwood parking lot, turn left onto an old road (clearing) and park at the end.

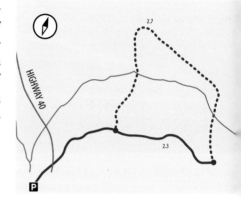

DISTANCE
4.6 km return

ELEVATION GAIN
250 m

DIFFICULTY
Moderate, recommended for children aged 6 and older. Good trail at the beginning and end. Faint to no trails in the middle of the loop route. Some route finding and boulder hopping necessary.

SEASON
Summer and early fall.

OF SPECIAL INTEREST FOR CHILDREN
Outstanding during larch season. Two idyllic streams may be the highlight for children.

1. The trail starts at the north end of the clearing and heads northeast, paralleling Arethusa Creek some distance away from it. Follow the trail as it gains elevation, ignoring any side trails.

2. Eventually the trail does fork, with one trail going across Arethusa Creek. *Do not* cross the creek. Instead, stay on the south side and on the trail that continues to parallel the creek, now heading east. The scenery is about to get excellent!

3. Follow the scenic creek up the valley. It soon disappears. Keep going, up a rock pile, towards the huge tower of rock in front of you.

4. A bench, the noticeably flatter area on the side of the mountain, appears below the tower, and that is where you want to go. Gain elevation up to the bench and then make a hard left (northwest) and follow the bench on faint trails in a generally northwest direction. This may be enough for younger families. Return the same way you came in.

en Stavric has made it to the bench (Courtesy Marko Stavric).

Going Farther: Complete the Loop
A superb extension of the Arethusa Cirque trip in sublime surroundings.

Distance
Add 2.7 km

Elevation Gain
Add 50–100 m

Difficulty
Moderately strenuous, recommended for children aged 8 and older. Off-trail travel, sometimes on rocky, loose terrain.

1. From the bench, stay above or around the treeline and hike all the way to the other side of the valley over to a small but stunningly beautiful creek that runs between Mount Arethusa and "Little Arethusa." The terrain underfoot around the creek is very fragile, so tread carefully. Follow the creek for as long as desired and then turn around, but on the west side of the creek.

2. The crux of the trip is finding the excellent trail that goes back to the main trail. The trail stays well above a large canyon-like feature where the creek runs. Hike south and down until you run into the trail, and then follow it down to where it intersects the creek you didn't cross earlier. Cross the creek and then return the same way you came in, back to your vehicle.

FACING PAGE FROM TOP Amélie and Aven Stavric at the bench. The loop route traverses above the treeline, at the far right, to the cirque below "Little Arethusa" (just right of centre) (Courtesy Marko Stavric); Looking back over the cirque and Storm Mountain; The idyllic stream and environs between "Little Arethusa" and Mount Arethusa. Tread carefully in this stunning but fragile environment.

11. PICKLEJAR LAKES

A fairly long hike to four beautiful lakes.

LOCATION

Drive west on Highway 1, then south on Highway 40 (Exit 118) for approximately 87 km (2 km past the Trout Ponds turnoff) to the Lantern Creek parking lot.

DISTANCE

10 km return for all four lakes

ELEVATION GAIN

615 m; high point: 2190 m

DIFFICULTY

Very strenuous, recommended for children aged 8 and older. Good trail throughout, with several steep sections and a rocky, slightly exposed descent to the lakes.

SEASON

Late spring, summer and early fall.

OF SPECIAL INTEREST FOR CHILDREN

Kids will probably like the side-hilling sections and then visiting all four lakes. Note the trail parallels Lantern Creek, not Picklejar Creek.

1. Cross Highway 40 to the east side and hike north alongside the road for a short distance to where the obvious trail veers right, into the forest.

2. Follow the well-worn trail, persevering through the first 20–30 minutes, when a big chunk of elevation is gained. The terrain eventually levels out a little for a long section and then another big elevation gain to the high point ensues.

3. The final section to the lakes involves a 60-m elevation loss down a rocky slope. There is a trail all the way, but you and the kids will want to watch your footing and descend with care. I've seen some kids run down this section, while others cling to their parents for dear life.

4. The first lake is quickly reached. Follow the trail around the south side of the first two lakes. The third lake has a trail around both sides. The best strategy may be to circle around the south (right) side of the third lake, continue on to the fourth lake, return to the third and then loop around the north side. The remainder of the return trip is the same way you came in.

CKWISE FROM TOP LEFT The reward for the first section of strenuous elevation gain is this view of ɘham Ridge. The Carreiro family also enjoys the levelling out of the trail at this point; Arika, Dan ₫ Josh Carreiro at the high point of the trail, just before it descends to the lakes; Looking down to third lake (Courtesy Off the Beaten Path, with Chris & Connie; BIGDoer.com).

Highway 1,
Bow Valley,
Canmore,
Highway 742
South

HIGHWAY 1, BOW VALLEY, CANMORE, HIGHWAY 742 SOUTH

Hikes around the eastern edge of the Rockies can be reached in just under an hour from the Calgary city limits. Those around Canmore take about an hour to reach, and most of the hikes along Highway 742 take 1.5–1.75 hours. Facilities and amenities are abundant in Canmore and, to a lesser degree, Exshaw.

The hikes in this section are generally more advanced than those in the same areas in Volume 1. Black Prince Cirque Interpretive Trail is good for beginners, whereas the Headwall Lakes trail will appeal to the seasoned young hiker.

12. YAMNUSKA TRAIL TO RAVEN'S END

Hike to the east side of one of the most iconic mountains in the Canadian Rockies.

LOCATION
Drive west on Highway 1 and take the Highway 1X turnoff towards Exshaw (Exit 114). Drive to the end of the road, turn right onto Highway 1A, go 2 km and turn left into the Yamnuska parking lot.

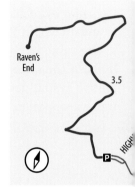

DISTANCE
7 km return

ELEVATION GAIN
520 m; high point: 1890 m

DIFFICULTY
Strenuous, recommended for children aged 6 and older. Good trail, with several steep sections.

SEASON
Late spring, summer and fall.

OF SPECIAL INTEREST FOR CHILDREN
Far-reaching views and then an inspiring visit to the impressive east side of Yamnuska. Perhaps "the carrot" that turns kids into scramblers.

1. From the end of the parking lot, follow the trail as it quickly crosses the road and then goes into light forest. Easy hiking is followed by a very steep grind to a signed junction.

2. Turn right and follow the hikers' trail. It is easy to follow, first traversing the southeast side of Mount Yamnuska and then turning left and going up the side of the mountain. Once some elevation is gained, a rock outcrop appears, providing a perfect rest spot and viewpoint.

3. Continue up the trail, keeping an eye out for a sharp left turn, marked by an arrow made from rocks. Take that trail and then follow your nose all the way to the steep walls of Yamnuska's east side. This is the end of the line for family hiking. Continuing beyond this point takes you into the realm of scrambling and is not recommended for young children. Return the same way you came in.

CKWISE FROM TOP Noah Koob takes in the view over the Bow Valley from the rock outcrop (Courtesy ya Koob); Penny Hobbs likes the far-reaching views too (Courtesy Matthew Hobbs); Follow the k arrow (Courtesy Karen Ung; playoutsideguide.com).

13. HA LING PEAK

A new and improved trail to one of the most popular viewpoints in the Rockies. A terrific advanced family hike.

LOCATION
Drive west on Highway 1 towards Canmore. Take the Three Sisters Parkway turnoff (Exit 93) and follow the 742 signs, eventually driving up a winding gravel road into the next valley. Just past Whiteman's Pond (at the top), drive down a hill and turn right, into the Goat Creek parking lot.

DISTANCE
6.8 km return

ELEVATION GAIN
700 m; high point: 2375 m

DIFFICULTY
Very strenuous, recommended for children aged 10 and older. Good, varied trail, but steep in places, with a significant amount of elevation gain. Note this route goes to the saddle between Ha Ling Peak and Miner's Peak, not the summit of either one. See Going Farther for those routes.

SEASON
Late spring, summer and fall.

OF SPECIAL INTEREST FOR CHILDREN
The kids will love the sense of accomplishment of reaching this significant viewpoint. Making it to the summit is icing on the cake.

1. From the parking lot, cross the road and find the Ha Ling trail. Cross the canal on a bridge and hike to the trail sign.

FROM LEFT The new steps. Avarie Rosteski follows her sister Holly and brother Ethan up; The kids at saddle.

2. Hike 3.3 km to the saddle and a "Trail Not Maintained" sign. Along the way, in addition to enjoying the new and very interesting trail, give the kids the "do not throw rocks" speech, regarding climbers coming up the other side of the mountain.

3. Upon reaching the "Trail Not Maintained" sign, scramble a short distance up to the ridge, where a magnificent viewpoint awaits. Return the same way you came in, or complete one of the extensions.

Going Farther: Ha Ling Peak
Older and more experienced kids will definitely want to continue to the summit of this significant peak.

Distance
Add 800 m return

Elevation Gain
Add 100 m; high point: 2475 m

FROM LEFT A look up to the summit from the saddle. Some people are taking the trail, others the ridge; The Skogen/Wong clan at the summit of Ha Ling Peak (Courtesy Amy Wong).

Difficulty

Very strenuous, recommended for children aged 12 and older. Scree trail and short sections of slab or steep rock.

1. From the saddle, the obvious summit sits to the north. Carefully follow the most prominent scree trail to the top. There are a few places where you have to cross slabs, but the rock is solid and grippy. Alternatively, follow the steeper, rocky ridge to the top. With good footwear, this is a fun route and less slippery than the scree. Remind the kids not to throw rocks when they reach the top and also to watch their step – it's a long fall down! There are several rock shelters and lots of room to explore at the summit. Return the same way you came in. If you did ascend the ridge, the scree trail may be an easier route for descent.

Going Farther: Miner's Peak

Easier than the summit of Ha Ling Peak and arguably with a better view.

Distance

Add 1.2 km return

Elevation Gain

Add 100 m; high point: 2475 m

Difficulty

Strenuous, recommended for children aged 10 and older. No trail and then an easy, primitive trail to the summit.

1. From the saddle, the summit sits to the south. Hike the generally wide ridge in that direction. A trail eventually appears and it's easy from there to the top. The summit is not huge and you'll want to watch your step. Enjoy terrific views of Ha Ling Peak, Canmore and Mount Lawrence Grassi to the south and then return the same way you came in.

2. Optional: For even more mountain fun, the small summit to the west can be reached in less than ten minutes from the summit of Miner's Peak. There is a trail. The last couple of moves to the small summit are more scrambling in nature but should be no problem for most kids. Return the same way you came in.

CKWISE FROM TOP LEFT From the saddle, Miner's Peak is the obvious rounded high point at the left. big peak is Mount Lawrence Grassi.; The grassy area between the saddle of Ha Ling and the mit of Miner's Peak provides Marggie Pitta, Danica Pitta, Noah Koob and Sebastian Pitta a great e to rest and take in the view of Ha Ling Peak (Courtesy Tanya Koob); The col between Miner's and summit to the west provides a great place for Ani Gleason, Alex and Xavier Winia, Noah Koob and ah Yawney to celebrate 800 m of elevation gain and a terrific view (Courtesy Tanya Koob).

14. WEST WIND PASS

Graduate the kids to a slightly higher level of hiking.
A steep grind but with great views.

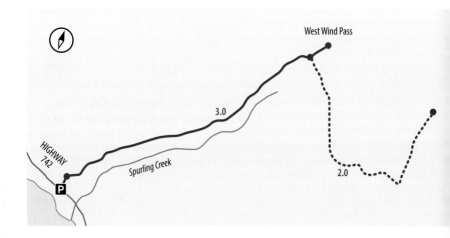

LOCATION

Drive west on Highway 1 towards Canmore. Take the Three Sisters Parkway turnoff (Exit 93) and follow the 742 signs, eventually driving up a winding gravel road into the next valley. Reset your odometer to zero upon reaching the Goat Creek parking lot. Drive about 13.2 km south on Highway 742 and park on the side of the road, near the dry drainage (1.6 km south of the Driftwood turnoff). Note this is not Spurling Creek but the next drainage to the northwest.

DISTANCE

6 km return

ELEVATION GAIN

375 m; high point: 2088 m

DIFFICULTY

Strenuous, recommended for children aged 8 and older. Good but varied trail throughout; a few narrow sections help keep your focus on footing.

FROM TOP Emi and Miya Ung, checking out Mount Lougheed from the trail (Courtesy Karen Ung; getoutsideguide.com); Grandpa (aka "GPA WONG," Bill Wong) demonstrates an impressive feat of strength with his granddaughters at the pass (Courtesy Amy Wong).

SEASON
Late spring, summer and fall.

OF SPECIAL INTEREST FOR CHILDREN

Sell this one to the kids as a tough workout to an amazing view-point with lots of terrain to explore when you get there.

1. Follow the signed trail (West Wind Valley) for about 150 m. Look for another steep trail veering up to the right and turn onto it.

2. For the next 2 km, simply follow this trail up to West Wind Pass, gaining 350 m of hard-earned elevation en route. If the kids start complaining ten minutes into the trip, you may want to change plans – the trail is relentlessly steep for most of the ascent.

3. Ignore all minor trails veering off to the left. About halfway up, the trail suddenly ends with slabs in front. A minor trail goes up to the left and another down to the right. Ignore both and cross the slabs to find the continuation of the trail. This happens again soon after.

4. About 200 m before reaching the pass, note the prominent trail veering off to the right – this is the Windtower Trail for those who are up for that challenge.

5. At the pass, there is much terrain to wander about and take in the wonderful views. You are sandwiched between the Rimwall to the northwest and the Windtower to the east. The grassy summit to the north is Wind Ridge. Return the same way you came in, or consider attempting the Windtower.

Going Farther: The Windtower

Definitely for older and more experienced kids. One of the more difficult trips in the book, with awesome views of Spray Lake.

Distance

Add 4 km return from West Wind Pass (10 km return from the highway)

Elevation Gain

616 m from West Wind Pass (975 m from the highway); high point: 2688 m

FROM LEFT There are several big cairns to mark the route; this energetic group of "youngsters" makes most of them. Typical terrain for the upper part of the ascent.

Difficulty
Very strenuous, recommended for children aged 12 and older. Interesting route finding and then steep scree to the top.

1. Go back to the junction mentioned in point 4 of the West Wind Pass hike on page 50.

2. Follow this new trail as it makes a long traverse across the west side of the Windtower towards the south ridge of the objective. The terrain along the traverse is interesting, mixing hiking and a little scrambling. There is also one mildly exposed section, so watch the kids here. There are many trails branching off – pick the most prominent one.

3. After traversing and going slightly up for about 0.8 km, a prominent trail branches off to the north. Make sure you pick the right trail that goes around and above a noticeable cliff band on your left side. Once on this trail it's an easy but long and foreshortened slog to the summit. Views of Spray Lake and Mount Lougheed will hopefully keep everyone entertained throughout the laborious ascent.

4. Be careful at the summit – it's a long way down if anyone slips. Enjoy the superb view and return the same way you came in.

15. HEADWALL LAKES

A more challenging and rewarding alternative to Chester Lake.
A stunning valley hike to two wonderful lakes.

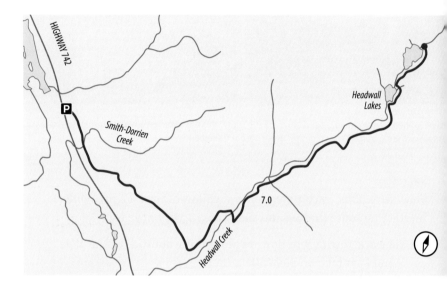

LOCATION

Drive west on Highway 1 towards Canmore. Take the Three Sisters Parkway turnoff (Exit 93) and follow the 742 signs, eventually driving up a winding gravel road into the next valley. Reset your odometer to zero upon reaching the Goat Creek parking lot. Drive about 36 km south on Highway 742 and turn left into the Chester Lake parking lot. Alternatively, drive west on Highway 1 and then drive south on Highway 40 (Exit 118) for 49 km to the Kananaskis Lakes turnoff. Turn right, drive 2.1 km and turn right again onto the Smith-Dorrien/Spray Trail (742). Drive 20 km and turn right, into the Chester Lake parking lot.

DISTANCE

14 km return

ELEVATION LOSS/GAIN

450 m; high point: 2340 m

pical scenery once the upper valley is reached.

DIFFICULTY
Very strenuous, recommended for children aged 12 and older. Varied terrain throughout, with steep rocky sections and a little scrambling.

SEASON
Summer and fall.

OF SPECIAL INTEREST FOR CHILDREN
This hike is for older kids who are up for a significant challenge. Biking the approach is also an option. There is lots of great water scenery, some scrambling, and fantastic views.

1. Find the trailhead signs at the south end of the parking lot. There are several trails that lead to the correct valley. Easiest is to follow the right fork of the Frost Heave trail. There is some elevation loss at the beginning. Hike the wide trail (old logging road) for several kilometres, ignoring all side trails.

2. Several kilometres along, the trail descends to Headwall Creek. Cross the creek on a wide bridge and continue up the other side, going up a steep hill in the opposite direction.

3. At the top of the hill, look for a narrow but obvious trail on the left side. This is the Headwall Lakes trail and will take you all the way to the lakes.

4. Follow the trail through varied terrain up the valley, always staying on the south (right) side of the creek.

5. Eventually arriving at an obvious boulder field, the trail goes around the left side.

6. Reaching another stand of trees and steep terrain, the trail now goes up alongside the trees for a very short distance and then turns left, into the trees. The steepest section of the trip is to follow. The trail neatly winds its way up through the trees to the rocky terrain above. Watch the kids carefully here.

7. Out in the open, the route to the lakes is very obvious, though the footing is a little more challenging on the rocky terrain.

8. Hike to the first lake, then around it on the east side and up a stunning headwall to the second lake. The cascading water separating the lakes is wonderful, but please be sensitive to its fragile environs.

9. If desired, hike to the north end of the second lake and then return the same way you came in.

FROM LEFT The first lake. Someone is fishing and others are taking in the scenery. The cascade at the back of the lake will be a hit with the kids (Courtesy Mark Fioretti); Mother and son (Michelle and Robbie Fioretti) reach the second lake (Courtesy Mark Fioretti).

16. WARSPITE LAKE/BLACK PRINCE CIRQUE

A pleasant forest walk to an interesting cirque and lake.

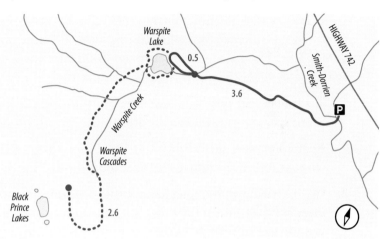

LOCATION

Drive west on Highway 1 towards Canmore. Take the Three Sisters Parkway turnoff (Exit 93) and follow the 742 signs, eventually driving up a winding gravel road into the next valley. Reset your odometer to zero upon reaching the Goat Creek parking lot. Drive about 48 km south on Highway 742 and turn right, into the Black Prince parking lot. Alternatively, drive west on Highway 1, then south on Highway 40 (Exit 118) for 49 km to the Kananaskis Lakes turnoff. Turn right, drive 2.1 km and then turn right again, onto the Smith-Dorrien/Spray Trail (742). Drive 8.3 km and turn left into the Black Prince parking lot.

DISTANCE

4.1 km return

ELEVATION GAIN

122 m; high point: 1820 m

DIFFICULTY

Moderate, recommended for children aged 4 and older. Good trail all the way.

SEASON
Late spring, summer and fall.

OF SPECIAL INTEREST FOR CHILDREN
There are lots of larches for the extension to Black Prince Lakes. By midsummer, Warspite Lake is more of a large puddle than a lake. Download the interpretive pamphlet: www.albert aparks.ca/media/125680/black_prince_cirque_trail__2_.pdf.

1. The trail is very easy to follow: over Smith-Dorrien Creek, up a long hill and gently down the other side.

2. At the junction, just after interpretive sign #5, go straight (the left fork is the return leg of the loop).

3. Upon arriving at Warspite Lake, either continue around the loop and then return the same way you came in, or continue the trip to Black Prince Lakes.

4. Optional: For added exercise and exploration, make your way around the rocky shores of Warspite Lake.

Going Farther: Black Prince Cirque and Black Prince Lakes
A very steep hike to a beautiful hanging valley, with the option to visit a few small tarns.

Distance
Add 5.2 km return

Elevation Gain
Add 400–500 m; high point: 2353 m

FACING PAGE, CLOCKWISE FROM TOP LEFT The Boora family, mum, Paula, and kids, Kiran, Naomi and Cass explore the fascinating rocky section of the trail just before reaching Warspite Lake (Courtesy Par Boora); The cascades are beautiful when a decent amount of water is flowing (Courtesy Matthew Clay); Warspite Lake, at high water, backdropped by Mount Black Prince. The route to Black Prince Cirque is at the left (Courtesy Matthew Clay); By August the lakes have dried up considerably. The ridge going from right to left provides terrific views; Arriving at the cirque. The distinctive form of Mount Warspite dominates the scene.

Difficulty

Very strenuous, recommended for children aged 12 and older. Good trail most of the way, with a boulder field to negotiate and some very steep terrain.

1. Hike around the left (south) side of Warspite Lake to the far west end and look for a trail that heads left into a stand of trees.

2. Go through the trees and follow the trail to a very noticeable field of rocks and boulders. Go over the boulder field – the footing here can be a little tricky, so use caution.

3. The trail resumes on the southwest side of the boulder field. Once beyond the next stand of trees, the route up to the hanging valley becomes more obvious.

4. Follow the increasingly steep terrain up to Warspite Cascades (a very scenic spot when a decent amount of water is flowing down the rock), and then up more steep terrain to the hanging valley.

5. The initial highlight of Black Prince Cirque is the towering form of Mount Warspite at the end of it. Continue into the valley until the full form of the mountain can be seen and decide what to do next. Some parties will call it a day here and return the same way they came in.

6. To get to Black Prince Lakes and a fine viewpoint, hike up the valley until the trees on your left peter out. The trail then turns right and ascends to a ridge above the small tarns.

7. Upon reaching the ridge, turn north and hike to its highest point. Watch the kids here, as there are places where a fall would have serious consequences. Take in the splendid view and then return the same way you came in.

17. SOUTH END OF LAWSON

A terrific summit, with outstanding views above the treeline.

LOCATION
Drive west on Highway 1, then south on Highway 40 (Exit 118) for 49 km and turn right on Kananaskis Trail. In 2.1 km, turn right, onto the Smith-Dorrien/Spray Trail (742), drive 2.9 km and turn right, onto an unsigned road. Park off to the side of the locked gate.

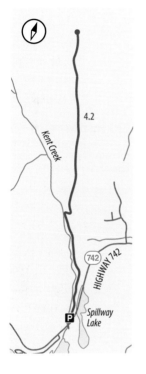

DISTANCE
8.4 km return

ELEVATION GAIN
690 m; high point: 2380 m

DIFFICULTY
Very strenuous, recommended for children aged 10 and older. Good trail throughout, with rocky and scrambly terrain near the summit. There are several sections of short but steep terrain and a little exposure.

SEASON
Late spring, summer and early fall.

OF SPECIAL INTEREST FOR CHILDREN
Your budding scramblers will love the rocky section near the summit. This is a good trip to do before tackling nearby and more challenging King Creek Ridge. Overall length and elevation gain are substantial.

1. Hike or bike the road north for 1.2 km to just before the dam and the end of the flume (V-shaped structure for transporting water) that reroutes Kent Creek.

2. About 20 m past the snowshoe sign, turn right and cross the dry creek onto a good trail.

3. Almost immediately, turn left up a steep trail. There ends the route finding. Once on this trail, simply follow it north to the summit, three horizontal kilometres and 690 vertical metres away. The trail is steepest right at the beginning and then becomes gentler. Higher up there are a couple of sections where you will want to keep an eye on the kids, as the drop on the right side gets quite serious. Finish the ascent with some scrambly terrain and then a short stint of hiking past a stand of trees to the summit. The view of Kananaskis Lakes is superb. Enjoy and then return the same way you came in.

CLOCKWISE FROM TOP LEFT Noah Koob hikes the approach road. South End of Lawson is dead ahead (Courtesy Tanya Koob); Finn Cohen and his dad, Alex, get above the treeline, where the view towards Kananaskis Lakes opens up (Courtesy Tanya Koob); Finn and his dad enjoy the section of f scrambling before the summit (Courtesy Tanya Koob).

Banff Area

BANFF AREA

The lure of Banff is easy to figure out: scenic hikes within short driving distances of one another, and then there's the townsite itself – no child can resist a visit to one of the town's candy stores! Go for a hike or two, stop for dinner and then end the day with a dip at the Banff Hot Springs – a perfect family outing. The feature hike in this area is spectacular Sunshine Meadows – bring your wallet, though, for the gondola.

Driving time from the city limits to Banff townsite is about 1.25 hours. Parking can be difficult to find on busy summer weekends, so expect to walk a little.

PREVIOUS PAGE Family hiking also includes soon-to-be families, as nine-months-pregnant Nicole Lisafeld proves. Husband, Brian Vale, and Mary the dog complete the picture.

18. MARSH LOOP

A relaxing trek alongside the famous Bow River, with two
optional and interesting side trips from the Cave and Basin.

LOCATION
Head west on Highway 1, take the Lake Minnewanka/Banff turnoff (Exit 69) and drive into Banff, down Banff Avenue and over
the Bow River. Turn
right and follow the
signs to the Cave and
Basin parking lot.

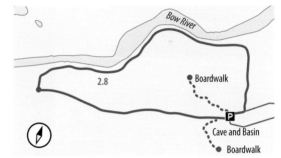

DISTANCE
2.8-km loop

ELEVATION GAIN
Minimal

DIFFICULTY
Easy, recommended for all. An excellent paved trail for the first
section, good trail for the loop. This path is stroller-friendly when
dry.

SEASON
Late spring, summer and fall.

OF SPECIAL INTEREST FOR CHILDREN
Visit the Cave and Basin National Historic Site before or after the
hike – it's free with your annual park pass.

1. The wide, paved path goes past the Cave and Basin and then
    gradually loses elevation down to the valley.

2. Follow the path for about 1 km and then turn right at the
    Marsh Loop trail sign.

3. Hike the loop, taking in excellent views of the Bow River and
    surrounding mountains.

CLOCKWISE FROM TOP LEFT Nine months pregnant and still getting out to the mountains. Mary the dog; Brian and Nicole on the bank of the beautiful Bow River; The final stretch of the hike grants good views of Mount Norquay; A curious youngster checks out the springs above the Cave and Basin; From the upper boardwalk, looking down on the Cave and Basin site, with Cascade Mountain behind (Courtesy Nicole Lisafeld).

4. The trail eventually takes a sharp turn to the right (south). Follow it straight back to the parking lot. Don't take the left turn as you near the parking lot.

5. Optional and Highly Recommended: The two boardwalk routes (one above the Cave and Basin and one below) are both interesting and educational.

19. SUNDANCE CANYON

Not quite the Grand Canyon, but wonderful nevertheless!
The approach is great for bikes.

LOCATION

Drive west on Highway 1, take the Lake Minnewanka/Banff turn-off (Exit 69) and drive into Banff, down Banff Avenue and over the Bow River. Turn right and follow the signs to the Cave and Basin parking lot.

DISTANCE

9 km return

ELEVATION GAIN

155 m

DIFFICULTY

Moderately difficult, recommended for children aged 6 and older. The wide, paved trail to the canyon is good for bikes. There are steep rock steps to ascend in the canyon.

SEASON

Spring, summer and fall.

OF SPECIAL INTEREST FOR CHILDREN

An excellent bike and hike for the family. There is terrific water scenery throughout. Can easily be combined with Marsh Loop. The canyon may be too challenging for small children.

1. Hike or bike past the Cave and Basin and follow the wide, paved trail down to the valley and then alongside the Bow River. There are good views of Mount Edith's south spire.

2. This trail eventually veers left and continues up to Sundance Canyon (well signed). A bike rack is available if you rode in.

3. Hiking the fascinating Sundance Canyon is a much steeper and more challenging affair for the young ones. Cross the creek on a bridge and follow the increasingly steep trail up the canyon. Steep rock steps are a feature of the trail.

4. Gain the upper canyon and continue following the trail through the flatter, but equally interesting, narrow valley.

5. The trail eventually ends up on the right side of the creek and soon veers to the right and up. Don't miss this turn.

6. Shortly after, there is a hairpin turn in the trail that heads back to the start of the canyon. Follow the trail through forest.

7. When the trail seems to end at a wooden fence, it actually curves way over to the left. Enjoy the switchbacking trail back to the start of the canyon. If you biked the approach, the ride back to the Cave and Basin parking lot will be a blast!

8. Optional: When you reach the turnoff to Marsh Loop, turn left and follow the trail as described on page 63.

CLOCKWISE FROM TOP LEFT Noah Koob and Ethan Mcdonough have wisely chosen to bike the approach (Courtesy Tanya Koob); Looking up Sundance Canyon (Courtesy Karen Ung; playoutsideguide.com); Miya Ung above the rock steps. These steps would be quite steep for a very young child (Courtesy Karen Ung; playoutsideguide.com).

20. SUNSHINE MEADOWS

An exciting trip for the family that starts with a gondola ride (or bus ride) and chairlift to the top. The environs of the "meadows" are sublime.

LOCATION
Drive west on Highway 1, past Banff. Take the Sunshine turnoff and follow the road 7 km to the Sunshine gondola.

DISTANCE
11.3-km loop

ELEVATION GAIN
160 m; high point: 2305 m

DIFFICULTY
Moderate, recommended for children aged 4 and older. Excellent trail throughout. Be sure to always stay on the trail.

SEASON
Summer and fall.

OF SPECIAL INTEREST FOR CHILDREN
There are many points of interest the kids will love, including tons of watery scenery, wildflowers by mid-July and far-reaching views. Check the internet for gondola ride prices ($42 adults, $21 children 6–16, free for toddlers 0–5 as of 2019). Bus rides are also offered on certain days. Sunshine Village has many amenities, including a lodge if you want to stay the night. Pick and choose your route. The description here is for the complete route.

1. Take the gondola up to Sunshine Village (20 minutes), grab a map at the top and then take the Standish chairlift to the high point of the day. With a map in hand, detailed instructions are not required, but the following is the suggested route to experience the area.

2. From the top of the chairlift, hike a short distance to the Standish Viewpoint for a fine view of the two lakes you will be visiting.

3. Hike 400 m down to an intersection and turn left towards Rock Isle Lake.

4. Another intersection is soon reached, but it is best to keep going straight to the Rock Isle Viewpoint on the northeast side of the lake.

5. Backtrack to the aforementioned intersection and turn left onto the trail that leads to the Larix Loop Trail. Hike 900 m to the start of the loop.

6. Hike the 2.5-km Larix Loop Trail in a clockwise direction. At the lake, views of the Monarch are terrific. The loop then continues on to Grizzly Lake and then to the Simpson Viewpoint. Although partially blocked by trees, Simpson Viewpoint offers a terrific view of the valley and the results of a forest fire.

7. Return to the first junction you reached. Instead of returning to the Standish Viewpoint, take the Twin Cairns to Monarch Lookout Trail going north. Hike 2.6 km to another signed junction.

8. Turn left and hike easily to the fine Monarch Viewpoint. If motivated, complete the extension described below in **Going Farther**, or return to the signed junction and then complete the loop via Meadow Park Trail. I'm sure the kids will want to pop into the Sunshine Village complex for treats at the end! Take the gondola back to the start.

M LEFT Grandpa (Bill Wong) and Mia Skogen on the Standish chairlift (Courtesy Amy Wong); Greg ...es and daughter, Leah, hike towards Rock Isle Lake (Courtesy Stacey Jones).

Going Farther: Simpson Pass
Some additional hiking for additional scenery around the Monarch Viewpoint.

Distance
Add 1.6 km return

Elevation Gain
Add 80 m on return

Difficulty
Strenuous, recommended for children aged 8 and older. Good trail throughout.

1. From the Monarch Viewpoint, continue on the trail towards Simpson Pass, losing elevation all the way.

2. Hike the trail for about 800 m until you arrive at a beautiful little stream characterized by orange-coloured rock. Stop here, cool off in the stream and then return to the Monarch Viewpoint. Going all the way to Simpson Pass is not very rewarding from a scenery standpoint and therefore not recommended.

FROM TOP Sunshine Meadows, page 67. More terrific scenery below Monarch Viewpoint; Stop here and then return to the viewpoint; Yes, there *is* ice cream at the end! Sisters Mera and Penny Hobbs share a tasty treat at Sunshine Village (Courtesy Matthew Hobbs).

Moraine Lake

MORAINE LAKE

Battling it out with Louise, Bow, Peyto, Kananaskis and Spray for lake supremacy in the Canadian Rockies is Moraine Lake – a deep-turquoise-hued body of water surrounded by a group of spectacular mountains known as the Valley of the Ten Peaks. No written description can ever prepare you for the sheer beauty of this lake.

Unfortunately, Moraine Lake, even more so than Lake Louise, has succumbed to the pitfalls of popularity, the most frustrating being accessibility. At present (2019), your options for getting to the lake during the summer months are to arrive at the parking lot before 5:30 am or pay $10 each to take a shuttle from the Lake Louise overflow (8 am – 4 pm). An online reservation system may be in place by 2020. The fee, in my opinion, is absolutely worth it. Expect large crowds at the lake and on most of the trails. Before you go, check for hiking restrictions due to bear activity.

Driving time from the Calgary city limits is usually at least 2.25 hours. Allow extra time if you are taking the shuttle. At the lake, Moraine Lake Lodge offers refreshments and meals. If your wallet is bursting at the seams, there is the option to stay at the lodge!

PREVIOUS PAGE Easy to see why Moraine Lake is a Canadian Rockies treasure.

21. MORAINE LAKE

*Combine with the Rockpile to get the most
out of your Moraine Lake experience.*

LOCATION
Drive west on Highway 1 to Lake Louise and follow the signs to
Moraine Lake. Note that the parking lot fills up as early as 6 am,
even on summer weekdays. On a busy weekend, the shuttle from
the Lake Louise overflow is your best bet ($10 each, but price may
vary).

DISTANCE
2.8 km return

ELEVATION GAIN
None

DIFFICULTY
Very easy, recommended
for all. Good trail, ending at
a platform.

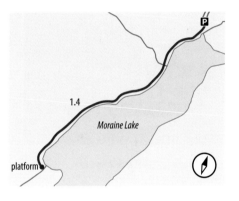

SEASON
Summer and early fall.

OF SPECIAL INTEREST FOR CHILDREN
After the hike, rent a canoe and explore the entire circumference
of the lake. Treats are available at Moraine Lake Lodge.

1. The well-signed trail simply follows the lakeshore for 1.4 km
    to a wooden platform. There are tons of photo opportunities
    along the way. Take your time and enjoy the ride, but do be
    respectful of other people and their hiking pace, especially
    when the trail is busy. Return the same way you came in.

CLOCKWISE FROM TOP LEFT Moraine Lake, page 73. Two minutes from your vehicle sits this view!; The water *really* is that colour! ("Why?" ask the kids. "The result of light refracting off the glacial silt suspended in the water," you answer; Amy Wong and Mia Skogen at the platform at the end of the trail (Courtesy Christian Skogen); Paddleboarding is one way to enjoy the lake and the magnificent mountains around it (Courtesy Mark Koob).

22. THE ROCKPILE

Picture-perfect views of the lake in less than ten minutes.

LOCATION
Drive west on Highway 1 to Lake Louise and follow the signs to Moraine Lake. Note that the parking lot fills up as early as 6 am, even on summer weekdays. On a busy weekend, the shuttle from the Lake Louise overflow is your best bet ($10 each, but price may vary).

DISTANCE
0.8 km return

ELEVATION GAIN
40 m

DIFFICULTY
Easy, recommended for all. Good trail with some steep steps. Stay on the trail throughout.

SEASON
Summer and early fall.

OF SPECIAL INTEREST FOR CHILDREN
The trail can get very congested. Be patient and respectful of others. Best combined with Moraine Lake and/or Consolation Lakes.

1. From the end of the parking lot the signed trail goes off to the left. Follow the signs up to the Rockpile (turning right a short ways in), explore the area (but stay on the trail), absorb the amazing views (in many directions) and return the same way you came in.

23. CONSOLATION LAKES

A pleasant forest walk to a gem of a lake,
surrounded by awe-inspiring, glaciated mountains.

LOCATION
Drive west on Highway 1 to Lake Louise and follow the signs to
Moraine Lake. Note that the parking lot fills up as early as 6 am,
even on summer weekdays. On
a busy weekend, the shuttle
from the Lake Louise overflow
is your best bet ($10 each, but
price may vary).

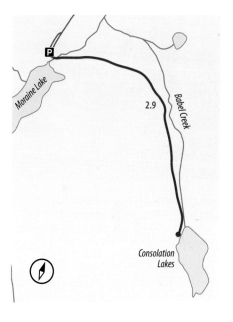

DISTANCE
5.8 km return

ELEVATION GAIN
120 m

DIFFICULTY
Moderate, recommended for
children aged 5 and older. Good
trail, with some boulder hopping and rocky terrain.

SEASON
Summer and early fall.

OF SPECIAL INTEREST FOR CHILDREN
Boulder hopping along the lakeshore can be fun for kids. Easily
combined with the Rockpile. Check for hiking restrictions (e.g.,
tight groups of four) due to bears in the area.

1. From the end of the parking lot the signed trail goes off to the
    left. Follow the trail past the Rockpile turnoff.

2. The trail goes across a boulder field and then into the forest –
    wonderfully cooling on a hot summer day. Good thing, as the
    trail gains about 120 vertical metres. Along the way there are

CLOCKWISE FROM LEFT Kaeli and soon-to-be-mother Brianne work their way through the boulder field just after the Rockpile (Courtesy Matthew Hobbs); Two climbers (Dan Carreiro and Mark Nugara) at Consolation Lake. The second lake is accessible but not recommended; Dan Carreiro and Mark Nug scramble over the boulders near the lakeshore. Mount Temple provides a pretty wild backdrop.

multiple opportunities to take little side trails to see Babel Creek on the left. Be patient and take one of the trails higher up that is easy and less steep.

3. The trail ends just before the actual lakeshore. Even here the views of awesome Mount Babel (towering over the west side of the lake) and glaciated Quadra Mountain are fantastic.

4. Scrambling over boulders to the lakeshore is the best way to fully experience the lake. However, be very careful if you choose to do so. Most of the boulders are quite stable, but the odd one will move or shift. There is a faint trail alongside the lake, but it is not recommended. Stay by the lake outlet and cool your feet in the icy water instead. Return the same way you came in.

24. LARCH VALLEY

Very simply a must-do hike at some point in your life!

LOCATION
Drive west on Highway 1 to Lake Louise and follow the signs to Moraine Lake. Note the parking lot fills up as early as 6 am, even on summer weekdays. On a busy weekend, the shuttle from the Lake Louise overflow is your best bet ($10 each, but price may vary).

DISTANCE
8.6 km return

ELEVATION GAIN
540 m; high point: 2425 m

DIFFICULTY
Strenuous, recommended for children aged 6 and older. Excellent trail throughout.

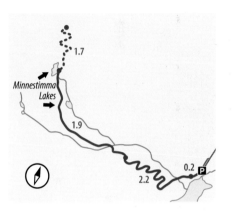

SEASON
Summer and early fall.

OF SPECIAL INTEREST FOR CHILDREN
Obviously a great larch season trip! Check for hiking restrictions (e.g., tight groups of four) due to bears in the area. Can be combined with Eiffel Lake but makes for a very long day.

1. The signed trailhead is at the north end of the parking lot. Follow the trail for 200 m to a signed junction. Turn right onto the Larch Valley/Minnestimma Lakes trail. Remember to check the sign to see if hiking in a tight group of four is recommended or mandatory.

2. Follow the trail for several kilometres up long switchbacks to another junction. Left goes to Eiffel Lake. Stay right and continue up to Larch Valley.

1. Get ready for great views of Eiffel Peak, Pinnacle Mountain and Mount Temple. Turning around allows you to see the

CLOCKWISE FROM TOP One of the most aesthetically beautiful scenes in the Rockies, and Shawn Benb... has captured it perfectly (Courtesy Shawn Benbow); Passing the upper Minnestimma Lake (Courte... Shawn Benbow); Leah and Stacy Jones returning from the valley, with Eiffel Peak and Pinnacle Mountain providing a stunning background (Courtesy Greg Jones).

magnificent Valley of the Ten Peaks. Follow the trail up to the small and shallow Minnestimma Lakes. Either return the same way you came in or continue on to Sentinel Pass.

Going Farther: Sentinel Pass
A steep grind up to a fine viewpoint.

Distance
Add 3.4 km return

Elevation Gain
Add 185 m; high point: 2610 m

Difficulty
Very strenuous, recommended for children aged 10 and older. Good but steep trail throughout.

1. The route is obvious. Follow the trail up several long switchbacks to the pass. You now get a view of the mountains on the north side, Lefroy being one of the more prominent ones. Of course, the view of the Ten Peaks and Minnestimma Lakes is probably going to be the highlight. Return the way same you came in. Note: Ascending Mount Temple is *not* a family hike – it's a very serious and difficult scramble for those with a ton of experience.

M LEFT The clearly defined zigzag trail up to Sentinel Pass (Courtesy Shawn Benbow); The Kitagawa nily at the pass. The view over the other side is pretty killer! (Courtesy Denise Kitagawa and family).

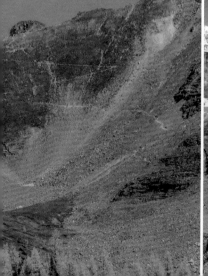

25. EIFFEL LAKE

A longer and less popular hike than Larch Valley,
but with stunning views of the Ten Peaks.

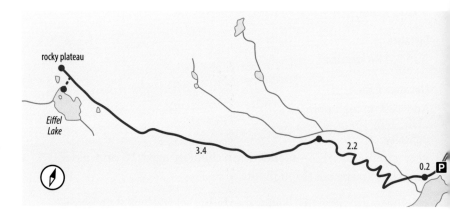

LOCATION
Drive west on Highway 1 to Lake Louise and follow the signs to
Moraine Lake. Note the parking lot fills up as early as 6 am, even on
summer weekdays. On a busy weekend, the shuttle from the Lake
Louise overflow is your best bet ($10 each, but price may vary).

DISTANCE
11.6 km return

ELEVATION GAIN
365 m; high point: 2255 m

DIFFICULTY
Strenuous, recommended for children aged 8 and older. Excellent
trail throughout.

SEASON
Summer and early fall.

OF SPECIAL INTEREST FOR CHILDREN
Excellent intermediate hike for kids, with a decent amount of
elevation gain and fantastic views. Check for hiking restrictions

Sweet views of some of the Ten Peaks accompany Amélie, Kyle and Emily as they hike around Eiffel Peak towards the lake (Courtesy Marko Stavric).

(e.g., tight groups of four) due to bears in the area. Steep snowbanks often spill across the trail well into the summer. Early-season attempts may be thwarted by snow. This hike can be combined with Larch Valley, but it makes for a very long day.

1. The signed trailhead is at the north end of the parking lot. Follow the trail for 200 m to a signed junction. Turn right onto the Eiffel Lake trail. Remember to check the sign to see if hiking in a tight group of four is recommended or mandatory.

2. Follow the trail for several kilometres up long switchbacks to another junction.

3. Turn left onto the Eiffel Lake trail and follow it around Eiffel Peak, high above the valley. Views improve dramatically throughout.

4. The goal is to hike a short distance past Eiffel Lake to the rocky plateau above it. Have a break and then return the same way you came in. Continuing on to Wenkchemna Pass is an option but makes for an almost 20-km day.

5. Optional: Scrambling down to the lake can be very rewarding, especially on a still day when lake reflections are possible. The best place to do so is about 150 m before the rocky plateau, where a rocky drainage runs down the mountain. There is a faint trail going down to the lake. Carefully descend the steep terrain to the lakeshore. Explore and then return the same way you came in.

FROM TOP The gang arrives at a viewpoint above Eiffel Lake (Courtesy Marko Stavric); On clear, calm days, the reward of getting down to the shores of Eiffel Lake can be breathtaking lake reflections.

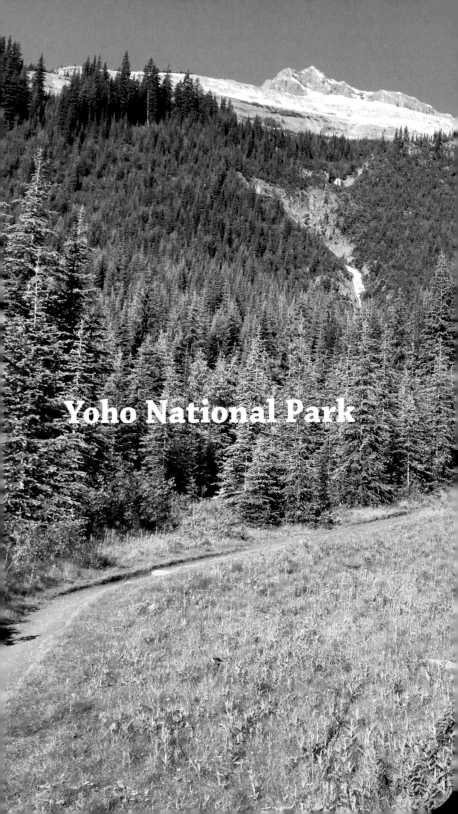

Yoho National Park

YOHO NATIONAL PARK

Stretching the upper limit of driving time for day trips (2.5 hours from Calgary), Yoho offers a number of fantastic hikes suitable for young kids. All amenities and a tourist information centre are available in the town of Field, about 30 km west of Lake Louise.

Unfortunately, the crown jewel of Yoho, Lake O'Hara, is difficult to access because of the requirement to make reservations months in advance. Therefore, trips in that area are not described in this book. There are several excellent family hikes in the Lake O'Hara area. Refer to Tony Daffern's *Popular Day Hikes: Canadian Rockies* for descriptions.

The other jewel of Yoho, Emerald Lake, thankfully is quite accessible (although often crowded on most summer weekends) and makes for a wonderful family hike.

Yoho is also home to Takakkaw Falls, the second-highest waterfall in Canada, an attraction that draws hikers and tourists from all corners of the globe. For those considering an extended stay near the falls, there is a walk-in campsite nearby and also a backcountry campsite at Laughing Falls.

Other camping options for the Yoho area include Hoodoo Creek, Kicking Horse and Monarch. Call 1-877-RESERVE for frontcountry campgrounds and 1-250-343-6783 for backcountry campgrounds.

PREVIOUS PAGE Lush forest, rugged mountains, and stunning glaciers are all part of the Yoho experienc

26. PAGET PEAK LOOKOUT

A great workout to an amazing viewpoint.

LOCATION
Drive 14.9 km past the Lake Louise turnoff and turn right, into the Sherbrooke Creek parking lot.

DISTANCE
7.8 km return

ELEVATION GAIN
520 m; high point: 2135 m

DIFFICULTY
Strenuous, recommended for children aged 7 and older. Good trail throughout, with rockier terrain higher up.

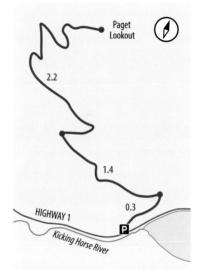

SEASON
Summer and early fall.

OF SPECIAL INTEREST FOR CHILDREN
A good physical challenge for younger kids. Making it to the lookout can provide good motivation. If things don't look good for the lookout en route, downgrade to Sherbrooke Lake.

1. From the trailhead, go up through the metal gate and then follow the trail for a few hundred metres. Turn left at the signed junction.

2. Continue on this trail for 1.4 km to another signed junction. Turn right, onto the Paget Lookout trail, and hike 2.2 km through forest and up switchbacks to the lookout. Enjoy the terrific views of Wapta Lake far below and glaciated Mount Victoria, as well as other views, and then return the same way you came in. Note that although the summit of Paget Peak is rated as an easy scramble, it is very steep and very loose. This extension is not recommended for families.

CLOCKWISE FROM TOP The trail and good views of Mount Ogden; This young family of five also went Sherbrooke Lake after the lookout trip – a very fit family!; Paget Lookout, with the steep, rocky slo of Paget Peak behind.

3. Optional: On return, if energy and motivation are still in abundance, follow the signs to Sherbrooke Lake (see next trip).

27. SHERBROOKE LAKE

A pleasant forest hike to a classic glacier-fed lake.

LOCATION
On Highway 1, drive 14.9 km past the Lake Louise turnoff and turn right, into the Sherbrooke Creek parking lot.

DISTANCE
6.6 km return

ELEVATION GAIN
165 m

DIFFICULTY
Moderate, recommended for children aged 5 and older. Good trail all the way, with a few steep sections and lots of tree roots.

SEASON
Summer and fall.

OF SPECIAL INTEREST FOR CHILDREN
A great introduction to more moderate hikes for the kids, without too much elevation gain.

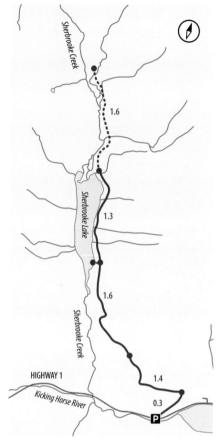

1. From the trailhead, go up through the metal gate and then follow the trail for a few hundred metres. Turn left at the signed junction.

2. Continue on this trail for 1.4 km to another signed junction. Keep going straight and hike 1.6 km to the lake. As you approach the lake, watch for a trail branching off to the left that goes to the lakeshore within a minute. Views of the lake and Mount Ogden above it are fantastic from this vantage

point. Return the same way you came in, or continue the trip to the north end of the lake (highly recommended).

3. Optional: 20 minutes of relatively easy hiking takes you to the north end of the lake. The trail does get a little narrow and exposed near the end. Views are excellent throughout.

Going Farther: North End of the Lake and Beyond
A waterfall and the pleasant meadows above are the draw here.

Distance
Add 2.6–5.8 km return

Elevation Gain
Minimal to the end of the lake; 85 m to the meadows

Difficulty
Easy to the end of the lake, moderately strenuous to the meadow; recommended for children aged 7 and older. Steep trail up to the meadow.

1. Simply follow the trail to the north end of the lake. It does get a little narrow, with a drop-off on the left side near the end.

2. Continue up the valley, as the steep trail starts up the headwall separating Sherbrooke Lake from the meadows above. The highlight of this section is a water cascade near the top. Watch the kids here – the drop-off is quite severe.

3. Eventually the trail emerges onto the open terrain of the valley above. Call it a day here or follow the trail to the north end of the valley. Two stream crossings (on log bridges) and great views make this a worthwhile trek if time and energy permit. Travel beyond the north end of the meadow gets tricky and makes for an extremely long day – it is therefore not recommended. Return the same way you came in.

CKWISE FROM TOP Kyle Kitagawa hikes the Sherbrooke shoreline (Courtesy Denise Kitagawa and *a*ily); Beautifully captured photo of the cascade (Courtesy Denise Kitagawa and family); The trail *i*s narrow towards the end of the lake (Courtesy Denise Kitagawa and family); Mount Ogden lies *a*oss the lake.

28. TAKAKKAW FALLS

the easiest yet most impressive hikes in the book.

LOCATION
On Highway 1, drive 22 km past the Lake Louise turnoff and turn right, onto Yoho Valley Road. Follow the road for 13 km to the Takakkaw Falls parking lot.

DISTANCE
1 km return

ELEVATION GAIN
Minimal

DIFFICULTY
Very easy, recommended for all. Paved trail all the way, with options to explore primitive trails closer to the falls.

SEASON
Summer and fall.

OF SPECIAL INTEREST FOR CHILDREN
You can get close enough to the falls to feel the spray. The boulders near the stream provide interesting scrambling. The main trail is stroller-friendly.

1. Hike the obvious paved path towards the falls, cross the bridge over the Yoho River and follow the path to its end.

2. There are many primitive trails that can get you closer to the falls, and the boulders by the river are great for exploration, but use discretion and keep an eye on the young ones. Back on the other side of the river, the red Adirondack chairs just south of the bridge make for good photo opportunities.

M LEFT The Koobs on the paved trail (Courtesy Mark Koob); Leah Jones has found a great spot
ve the trail to get close to the falls (Courtesy Greg Jones).

29. YOHO LAKE

Escape the crowds and enjoy a rewarding hike
to a pristine alpine lake.

LOCATION

On Highway 1, drive 22 km past the Lake Louise turn-off and turn right, onto Yoho Valley Road. Follow the road for 13 km to the Takakkaw Falls parking lot.

DISTANCE

9.8 km return

ELEVATION GAIN

290 m

DIFFICULTY

Strenuous, recommended for children aged 7 and older. Good trail all the way.

SEASON

Summer and early fall.

OF SPECIAL INTEREST FOR CHILDREN

Recommended for older kids who are used to long forest walks and fairly steep sections of trail. The kids will probably enjoy the lake and the Going Farther option even more.

1. From the parking lot, hike towards Takakkaw Falls but do not cross the bridge. Hike past the Adirondack chairs and follow the connector trail that soon crosses the road and leads to the Whiskey Jack Hostel. The signed trailhead is reached just before the hostel. Note that this point is considered to be the Takakkaw Falls parking lot, in reference to the distances on the signs.

sy walking and good views to start the trip.

2. Hike 1.1 km to the first junction. A big chunk of the elevation is gained here and there are occasional good views of Takak-kaw Falls.

3. At the first junction, a side trip to the two Hidden Lakes is optional (600 m return). The second lake is quite pretty, though no one is about to be "blown out of the water"!

4. From the first junction, another 200 m takes you to the second. Go straight.

5. About 2.7 km of generally easy hiking takes you to Yoho Lake. There are numerous points along the west shore to get good views. Hike past the campground to the red Adirondack chairs on the northwest side of the lake for the best views. Return the same way you came in, or make a loop of it as described below (highly recommended).

Going Farther: The Loop via Highline Trail
Amazing open views for the small price of some additional elevation gain and a little extra distance.

Distance
Add an additional 1.5 km to the return trip

FROM LEFT Decent views of Michael Peak from the south end of Yoho Lake; Wapta Mountain towers above Yoho Lake.

Elevation Gain
Add 135 m

Difficulty
Strenuous, recommended for children aged 8 and older. Good trail most of the way, with a few rocky sections.

1. Go to the Yoho Lake campground and find the food hanger. From there, hike the trail that goes north. Follow it for 2.4 km to the next junction. Once above the treeline, the views to the east over Waputik Icefield are outstanding.

2. At the junction, turn right and follow the signs back to the Takakkaw Falls parking lot.

On the Highline Trail, just before the view really starts to open up

30. ICELINE TRAIL

*A tough but thrilling hike to the stunning and
barren environs of Emerald Glacier.*

LOCATION

On Highway 1, drive 22 km
past the Lake Louise turnoff and turn right, onto
Yoho Valley Road. Follow
the road for 13 km to the
Takakkaw Falls parking lot.

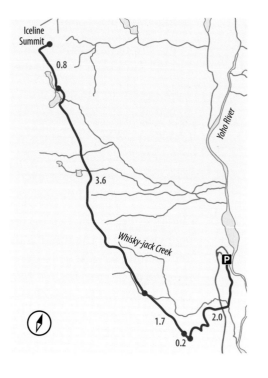

DISTANCE

14.6 km return

ELEVATION GAIN

685 m; high point: 2210 m

DIFFICULTY

Very strenuous, recom-
mended for children aged
12 and older. Steep, rocky
trail once above the treeline,
with a few narrow sections.

SEASON

Mid-July to early fall.

OF SPECIAL INTEREST FOR CHILDREN

Perhaps the kids' first close-up look at a glacier. Lots of room for
exploration.

1. From the parking lot, hike towards Takakkaw Falls but do not
   cross the bridge. Hike past the Adirondack chairs and follow
   the connector trail that soon crosses the road and leads to
   the Whiskey Jack Hostel. The signed trailhead is reached just
   before the hostel. Note that this point is considered to be the
   Takakkaw Falls parking lot, in reference to the distances on
   the signs.

2. Hike 1.1 km to the first junction. A big chunk of the elevation is gained here and there are occasional good views of Takakkaw Falls.

3. At the first junction, a side trip to the two Hidden Lakes is optional (600 m return). The second lake is quite pretty, though no one is about to be "blown out of the water"!

4. From the first junction, another 200 m takes you to the second. Turn right towards the Iceline Trail.

5. Hike 1.7 km to the next junction and take the right fork, as signed.

6. It's about 3.6 km, across the wild moraines below what's left of Emerald Glacier, to the next signed junction. The kids will probably enjoy hopping over the numerous small streams running down from the glacier.

7. The junction sits by two beautiful glacial tarns – one of the big highlights of the trip. Keep going straight, past the tarns, and then turn right, up to the obvious high point, commonly referred to as the Iceline Summit. It's about 800 m from the junction to the summit. Return the same way you came in. From the tarns, there is the option is visit Celeste Lake and then return via Laughing Falls. This option makes for a 19-plus-km day and is not recommended as a family hike.

FACING PAGE, CLOCKWISE FROM TOP Once above the treeline, views to the east and northeast are stunning (Courtesy Denise Kitagawa and family); Lots of streams running down from the receding glacier (Courtesy Denise Kitagawa and family); Passing the third tarn and heading to the Iceline Summit in the centre (Courtesy Denise Kitagawa and family); At times the trail is simply walking across smooth slabs of glacially eroded rock (Courtesy Denise Kitagawa and family).

31. LAUGHING FALLS

A somewhat dull approach, but the impressive destination makes it worthwhile. A good candidate for a first backcountry camping trip.

LOCATION
On Highway 1, drive 22 km past the Lake Louise turn-off and turn right, onto Yoho Valley Road. Follow the road for 13 km to the Takakkaw Falls parking lot.

DISTANCE
8.8 km return

ELEVATION GAIN
130 m

DIFFICULTY
Moderate, recommended for children aged 6 and older. Good trail all the way, with one lengthy section of steep uphill.

SEASON
Summer and fall.

OF SPECIAL INTEREST FOR CHILDREN
Lots of great water scenery, especially if you complete the side trips.

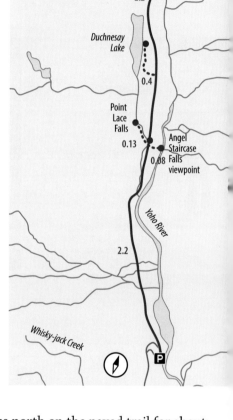

1. From the parking lot, hike north on the paved trail for about 500 m, past the Takakkaw Falls campground to the signed trailhead.

Greta and Makenna Duncan, and Noah and Mark Koob are on their way to Laughing Falls Campground (Courtesy Tanya Koob); Tanya and Noah Koob at the falls (Courtesy Mark Koob).

2. About 1.7 km of easy trail takes you to the first intersection. Angel's Staircase Falls viewpoint is about 80 m on the trail to the right. Point Lace Falls viewpoint is about 130 m on the trail to the left. Both viewpoints are easy to reach and recommended at this point or on return.

3. The next 2.2 km to Laughing Falls involves a steep climb and then a gradual descent back down to the river. As you approach the falls, there are a few points where you can get close to the always-raging river. Be very careful if you choose to do so, as a slip into the fast-flowing river would probably be fatal.

4. After crossing the Little Yoho River on a bridge, the Laughing Falls Campground is reached, with Laughing Falls only a minute upstream. The trail does get close enough to the falls for the kids to get wet from the spray. Don't go beyond this point. Return the same way you came in. Note the 400-m detour to see Duchesnay Lake if you want a little extra exercise and a decent view of an interesting lake.

32. EMERALD LAKE

A wonderful hike around a superbly colourful lake.
One of the many true gems of Yoho.

LOCATION
From Highway 1, 1.6 km west of the
Field turnoff, take the turnoff to
Emerald Lake and follow the road to
the parking lot.

DISTANCE
5.3-km loop

ELEVATION GAIN
Minimal

DIFFICULTY
Easy, recommended for all. Excellent semi-paved trail for much of the
loop; good mud-packed trail for the
rest.

SEASON
Late spring, summer and early fall.

**OF SPECIAL INTEREST FOR
CHILDREN**
After the hike, rent a canoe to
explore the lake. Stop at the geo-
logically interesting Natural Bridge when driving back along the
approach road. Get there early to beat the crowds.

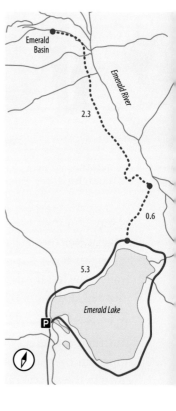

1. Hike down towards the lake and find the wide, paved trail
    that starts going around it in a clockwise direction. While the
    trail isn't right on the lakeshore throughout, there are many
    spots to enjoy great views of the lake, as well as take breaks
    if necessary. Along the north shore there are several minor
    trails that take you right to the lake, with excellent views of
    the entire area.

FROM LEFT The Benbow family and the lake, whose name is fairly obvious (Courtesy Shawn Benbow); humans aren't the only life form to enjoy the beauty of the lake.

2. Stay to the right throughout the loop, ignoring the horse trails and other turnoffs, unless you plan to tackle Emerald Basin (see **Going Farther**). Approaching the end of the 5.3-km loop an intersection is reached. Left goes directly to the parking lot and right goes through the Emerald Lake Lodge area. With kids in tow, right may be your best bet! Snacks and beverages are available.

Going Farther: Emerald Basin
A far more intense affair than the Emerald Lake loop. It gets you up to a stunning alpine basin with two waterfalls. This hike definitely favours a bluebird day. A great trail but relentlessly steep for several sections.

Distance
Add 5.8–6.8 km return

Elevation Gain
Add 225 m; high point: 1540 m

Difficulty

Very strenuous, recommended for children aged 12 and older. Good trail most of the way, with a few steep sections and rocky terrain near the waterfalls.

1. The signed turnoff is 2.1 km from the start of the Emerald Lake trail (in a clockwise direction). Turn left onto it and hike 600 m to another sign.

2. Turn left onto the new trail and follow it 2.3 km to the basin. On a clear day, the views of sections of the President Range are incredible.

3. Optional: For those who are comfortable on loose, rocky terrain without a trail, it's possible to hike right up to the obvious dual waterfalls towards the left side of the basin. Return the same way you came in.

CLOCKWISE FROM TOP Spectacular Emerald Basin. Note the dual waterfalls at the left; The Natural Bridge; Up close with the left-hand waterfall.

33. WAPTA FALLS

A long drive but a short hike to an amazing waterfall.

LOCATION
Drive west on Highway 1, past Lake Louise and Field. Look for the turnoff to Chancellor Peak Campground but don't turn there. Drive about 900 m past the Chancellor Peak Campground turnoff and turn left onto an unsigned gravel road. Drive the gravel road 1.7 km to the trailhead.

DISTANCE
1.8 km return

ELEVATION LOSS/GAIN
60 m

DIFFICULTY
Moderate, recommended for children aged 4 and older. Good trail all the way to the falls. Opportunity for off-trail exploration around the falls.

SEASON
Late spring, summer and early fall.

OF SPECIAL INTEREST FOR CHILDREN
Take a raincoat if you want to get close to the falls. The kids will probably want to climb the "hills" in front of the falls – use discretion if you let them. Given the lengthy driving time (approximately 2.75 hours from Calgary), this is best combined with another trip, such as Emerald Lake, or as a stop-off on the way to Golden.

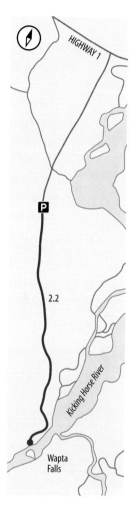

1. Hike the easy, relatively flat trail for about 1.5 km. The trail then gently ascends to a fenced viewpoint above the falls. Note the two "hills" by the falls that offer close-up views.

2. From the first viewpoint, descend the trail, taking a left turn almost right away and arriving at another viewpoint in short order. Going straight at the aforementioned intersection leads to the falls eventually but misses another viewpoint. This route is not as steep as the left-turn route.

3. Continue down to the falls. There is lots of room to explore this area and take in the terrific views. Note the following:
    - Expect to get drenched from the spray if you get close to the falls. Leave all electronic devices a good distance away.
    - The terrain around the falls can be very slippery, steep and dangerous. Proceed with extreme caution.
    - The second "hill" provides an excellent viewpoint but is very slippery to ascend and descend.
    - A small sandy area a short distance downstream is a great place for lunch.

4. Return the same way you came in. Taking the less steep trail is an option here.

CLOCKWISE FROM TOP LEFT Noah Koob has chosen a Strider as his mode of transportation for the approach (Courtesy Tanya Koob); Shawn and Jennifer Benbow enjoy the winter view of the falls (Courtesy Shawn Benbow); Looking down on the falls from one of the upper viewpoints. Note that winter trips to the falls are quite possible and very scenic (Courtesy Shawn Benbow).

Icefields Parkway (Highway 93 North)

ICEFIELDS PARKWAY (HIGHWAY 93 NORTH)

Let's go camping! Described as one of the most scenic drives in the world, the stretch of highway between Lake Louise and Jasper is not to be missed. And given the lengthy driving time from any major centre, the best and most logical way to experience the parkway is to spend a night or two or three at one of the many campgrounds along the way: Mosquito Creek, Silverhorn Creek and Waterfowl Lake for the southern section; Rampart Creek, Wilcox Creek, Columbia Icefields, Jonas Creek, Honeymoon Lakes, Mount Kerkeslin, Pocahontas, Wabasso and Wapiti for the northern section – book online and book early!

This volume of *Family Walks and Hikes* includes two trips on the southern half of the highway, which can be reached in about 2.5 hours from Calgary, and five trips on the northern half, each necessitating a drive time of about 3.5–4.5 hours one way. If the kids are getting restless during the drive, the parkway offers numerous scenic stops along the way for everyone to stretch their legs. These include Herbert Lake, Crowfoot Glacier, Bow Lake, Waterfowl Lakes and Tangle Falls.

There are no amenities on the southern half of Highway 93 North. Stop at Lake Louise if needed. Saskatchewan River Crossing, halfway between Lake Louise and Jasper, offers lodging, food and gas. The town of Jasper offers all amenities.

PREVIOUS PAGE A family of five enjoys one of the premier views in all of the Rockies from Wilcox Ridge

34. HELEN LAKE

Strenuous but superb hike to a beautiful alpine lake
amid stunning mountain scenery.

LOCATION
Drive west on Highway 1, past Lake Louise, and take the Highway 93 turnoff (Exit 7) towards Jasper. Drive about 33 km and turn right, into the Helen Lake parking lot.

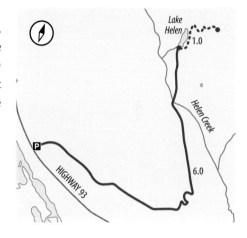

DISTANCE
12 km return

ELEVATION GAIN
455 m

DIFFICULTY
Strenuous, recommended for children aged 8 and older. Good trail, but tree roots and rocks throughout.

SEASON
Summer and fall.

OF SPECIAL INTEREST FOR CHILDREN
Good chance to see hoary marmots, in addition to the lake. Great in late July and early August, when the wildflowers are out.

1. From the trailhead, simply follow the Helen Lake trail for 6 km to the lake. A few of the side trails offer decent views over Bow Lake but are not necessary to visit. Once the trail swings around the hillside, views improve dramatically and get even better as you make your way up the valley. Note the signs urging all to stay on the designated trails. Enjoy the lake and then either return the same way you came in or complete the highly recommended extension.

CLOCKWISE FROM TOP LEFT Early morning mist doesn't always fill the valley, but it's cool when it does; Raff the mountaineer approaches a scenic creek crossing before the lake; Helen Lake is wonderful backdropped by Cirque Peak, a terrific scramble for when the kids are grown-up.

Going Farther: Helen Ridge
Amazing views everyone will want to experience.

Distance
Add 2 km return

Elevation Gain
Add 120 m; high point: 2520 m

Difficulty
Very strenuous, recommended for children aged 10 and older. Good trail, quite steep in places.

1. Follow the obvious trail around the east side of Helen Lake and then up to the ridge above the lake. As expected, views of the surrounding area are spectacular. Return the same way you came in.

M TOP Don't forget to turn around as you e the east shore of the lake; The fascinating k folding of the southeast face of Cirque k is one of many scenic rewards for making the ridge; The view from the ridge now udes glaciated Crowfoot Mountain.

35. MISTAYA CANYON

y hike down to a remarkable water-eroded canyon.

LOCATION

Drive west on Highway 1, past Lake Louise, and take the Highway 93 turnoff (Exit 7) towards Jasper. Drive about 70 km and turn left into the Mistaya Canyon parking lot.

DISTANCE
0.6 km return

ELEVATION LOSS/GAIN
60 m

DIFFICULTY
Very easy, recommended for all. A good trail down to the canyon. Off-trail travel at the shore of the river.

SEASON
Late spring, summer and fall.

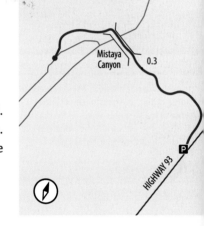

OF SPECIAL INTEREST FOR CHILDREN
Short, easy and spectacular. Watch the kids carefully if you choose to go down to Mistaya River.

1. From the trailhead, hike about 300 m down to the bridge over the canyon and enjoy the views from the bridge. Pre-warn the kids about the dangers of falling into the canyon and hold hands if need be.

2. Optional: Follow the trail on the other side of the bridge that goes down to the mighty Mistaya River. Be *very* careful about getting too close to the edge. There is flat, stable rock a short ways upstream where the kids can enjoy the rushing water.

CLOCKWISE FROM TOP Part of the canyon, as seen from the bridge; Hiking a short distance upstream offers some different scenery; The rock on the west side of the river provides a great viewpoint – ju don't get too close; Looking down the canyon from the west side.

36. PARKER RIDGE

A relatively short hike to a fabulous viewpoint overlooking the mighty Saskatchewan Glacier.

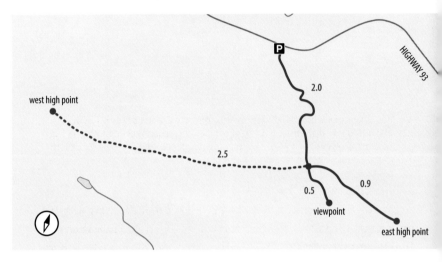

LOCATION
Drive west on Highway 1, past Lake Louise, and take the Highway 93 turnoff (Exit 7) towards Jasper. Drive about 117 km and turn left into the Parker Ridge parking lot.

DISTANCE
5.8–6.8 km return

ELEVATION GAIN
320 m; high point: 2320 m

DIFFICULTY
Moderate, recommended for children aged 5 and older. Good trail all the way (stay on it throughout to avoid damaging the fragile environment).

SEASON
Summer and early fall (snow patches may persist well into July).

ABOVE, FROM LEFT Brianne with baby, dad Matt, Crux the dog and Grandma (aka Pat Hobbs) on the wonderful trail. Mount Athabasca is a constant companion (Courtesy Gordon Hobbs); Nicole Hasafeld checks out the Saskatchewan Glacier and Castleguard Mountain. BELOW The Hobbs clan approaches the east summit (Courtesy Matthew Hobbs).

OF SPECIAL INTEREST FOR CHILDREN

Great views requiring minimal effort. Let the kids know why it's important to stay on the trail in this fragile area. Note that this trail is prone to closure in late spring in order to protect the delicate environment.

1. From the signed trailhead, follow the well-trodden trail up through several switchbacks to the ridge, about 2 km from the start.

2. From the ridge, you can descend a short distance (about 500 m) down the other side for terrific views of the Saskatchewan Glacier and/or continue following a minor trail as it veers left (east) towards the obvious east high point about 900 m away. Return the same way you came in, or do the extension to the west high point.

FROM LEFT Tanya and Noah Koob head towards the west high point (Courtesy Mark Koob); Approaching the west high point at the far right (Courtesy Mark Nugara).

Going Farther: West High Point
For even better views and extra exercise.

Distance
Add 5 km return

Elevation Gain
Add 200–320 m; high point: 2600 m

Difficulty
Strenuous, recommended for children aged 7 and older. Faint trail and off-trail travel to the high point.

1. From the east high point, start by returning the way you came and simply continue going west towards the other obvious high point along the ridge.

2. It's up to you how far you go. The farthest point would be the significant summit about 2.5 km from the low point. It gets fairly steep towards the top. This summit is for experienced families only. After enjoying another magnificent view, return the same way you came in.

37. WILCOX PASS

The big brother of Parker Ridge. Outrageously stunning
views of the Athabasca Glacier and mountains of
the Columbia Icefield. Another must-do route.

LOCATION
Drive west on Highway 1, past Lake Louise, and take the Highway
93 turnoff (Exit 7) towards Jasper. Drive about 123 km and turn
right, into the Wilcox Creek Campground. Park at the trailhead
kiosk, a short distance up the road.

DISTANCE
6.8 km return

ELEVATION GAIN
320 m; high point:
2375 m

DIFFICULTY
Strenuous, recom-
mended for children
aged 6 and older.
Good trail through-
out, with a few steep
sections.

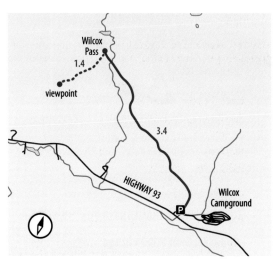

SEASON
Midsummer and early fall (snow patches may persist well into
July).

OF SPECIAL INTEREST FOR CHILDREN
Perhaps the kids' first experience seeing heavily glaciated
mountains.

1. Hike the steep trail through forest and on a short boardwalk
    eventually out onto an open ridge.

2. Continue in a northwest direction, enjoying the increasingly
    terrific view to the west. Ignore the side trails. The pass is

CLOCKWISE FROM TOP The Adirondack chairs provide a perfect viewpoint and rest stop for Brianne an Mera Hobbs (Courtesy Matthew Hobbs); Mother and son and one of the premier views in the Rock (Courtesy Mark Koob); Noah Koob leads his dad, Mark, up the trail (Courtesy Tanya Koob).

marked with a sign. Return the same way you came in, or complete the highly recommended traverse over to Wilcox Ridge.

Going Farther: Wilcox Ridge
The "must-do" part of a must-do route.

Distance
Add 2.8 km return

Elevation Gain
Add 100 m; high point: 2420 m

Difficulty
Strenuous, recommended for children aged 6 and older. Good trail, but several short steep sections.

1. Simply follow the well-marked trail up and over a few bumps to one of the finest viewpoints in the Rockies. Drink up the awe-inspiring views and then return the same way you came in.

TO BOTTOM The trail is easy to follow; Mounts Athabasca and Andromeda and the rapidly receding habasca Glacier are the highlights of the view.

38. FOREFIELD TRAIL/TOE OF THE ATHABASCA GLACIER

Two short hikes that can be combined for a
terrific overview of the Columbia Icefields area.

LOCATION
Drive west on Highway 1, past Lake Louise, and take the Highway 93 turnoff (Exit 7) towards Jasper. Drive about 126 km and turn left into the Athabasca Glacier parking lot. Park in either the Forefield parking lot (described below) or the Toe of the Glacier parking lot.

DISTANCE
5.4 km return

ELEVATION GAIN
50 m

DIFFICULTY
Easy, recommended for children aged 5 and older. Rocky trail and a few steep sections.

SEASON
Late spring, summer and early fall.

OF SPECIAL INTEREST FOR CHILDREN
Note: These trails can also be done individually. Perhaps someone can convince mum or dad to retrieve the car from the Forefield parking lot and drive down to the Toe of the Glacier parking lot to pick everyone up!

1. From the Forefield parking lot (recommended because it sports a glorious view of Mount Athabasca, whereas the Toe of the Glacier parking lot does not), hike the wide, paved trail west. The trail soon shrinks to a rocky, narrow, single-track trail.

2. Follow the trail as it winds through the rocky terrain, over a stream (log bridge) and then gradually descends to the Toe of the Glacier parking lot. Take your time and enjoy the changing views and amazing glacier scenery.

3. Optional and Highly Recommended: Hike the well-marked and signed Toe of the Glacier trail for excellent views of the Athabasca Glacier. For everyone's safety, stick to the trail and

TO BOTTOM Couldn't ask for a better starting view than this; Some of the Forefield trail is lined rocks to help you find your way. The Collins family from England didn't get the best weather, at least there's a faint rainbow above; The markers that show the rapid retreat of the glacier shocking.

2006

39. SUNWAPTA FALLS

little stop to stretch the legs and see several waterfalls.

LOCATION
Drive west on Highway 1, past Lake Louise, and take the Highway 93 turnoff (Exit 7) towards Jasper. Drive about 175 km and turn left into the Sunwapta Falls parking lot.

DISTANCE
2.8 km return

ELEVATION LOSS/GAIN
87 m loss/gain for the Lower Falls

DIFFICULTY
Very easy for the Upper Falls, easy for the Lower Falls, recommended for all. Good trail throughout. For safety, always stay behind the fences.

SEASON
Late spring, summer and fall.

OF SPECIAL INTEREST FOR CHILDREN
Not as spectacular as Athabasca Falls, but the hike down to the Lower Falls provides some good exercise for the young ones.

1. The Upper Falls is only minutes from the parking lot. Check it out from the bridge and both ends of the bridge, staying behind the fences.

2. The Lower Falls is easily reached via a signed trail on the north side of the Sunwapta River. Follow the descending trail as far down as the fences go and then return the same way you came in.

FACING PAGE, TOP TO BOTTOM One of the several small cascades of the Lower Falls; The Upper Falls and the fence that prevents kids from getting too close..

40. ATHABASCA FALLS

...pectacular waterfall only minutes from the parking lot.

LOCATION
Drive west on Highway 1, past Lake Louise, and take the Highway 93 turnoff (Exit 7) towards Jasper. Drive about 198 km, turn left onto Highway 93A and go to the Athabasca Falls parking lot.

DISTANCE
1 km return

ELEVATION GAIN
Minimal

DIFFICULTY
Very easy, recommended for all. Excellent paved trail and some easy steps.

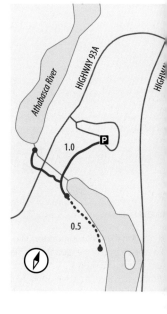

SEASON
Late spring, summer and fall.

OF SPECIAL INTEREST FOR CHILDREN
The kids will probably like the side trip down to the river below the falls.

1. Follow the well-marked trail to all of the viewpoints of the magnificent falls. Obviously, you'll want to keep an eye on the small ones here.

2. Be sure to visit the signed "Canyon," "River" and "Pothole" for additional views.

3. Optional: To extend the trip a little, and perhaps escape the crowds, hike the trail on the other side of the river that goes upstream. Eventually the trail narrows and starts going up the embankment. This is a good place to stop, take a break and then return the same way you came in.

M TOP Athabasca Falls, wonderfully
kdropped by picturesque Mount Kerkeslin
urtesy Shawn Benbow); Kate Collins at
Athabasca River; Another good place
kids to observe the spectacle. Clearly,
ter Benbow is impressed (Courtesy
wn Benbow).

Jasper

JASPER

The quaint town of Jasper is surrounded by spectacular mountain scenery and therefore a variety of wonderful hikes, many of which are appropriate for the whole family. Nearby Maligne Lake is a family favourite, featuring the easy but awe-inspiring Maligne Canyon hike and more advanced hikes (Opal Hills and Bald Hills). Just south of the townsite, the Valley of the Five Lakes is recommended for younger families.

Accommodations are plentiful in Jasper, though you'll want to book well in advance. For campers, the Wapiti, Whistler (family-oriented and highly recommended) and Snaring campgrounds provide a less expensive alternative.

Note that dogs are not allowed on the trails in Jasper, in order to protect the endangered caribou population.

NG PAGE Jennifer, James and Shawn Benbow at the lower viewpoint of Cavell Meadows (Courtesy wn Benbow).

41. VALLEY OF THE FIVE LAKES

..great hike to five gorgeous lakes – a family favourite.

LOCATION
From Jasper, drive 8.8 km south on Highway 93 and turn left into the Valley of the Fives Lakes parking lot. If arriving from the south, the turnoff is about 21.6 km north of the turnoff to Athabasca Falls.

DISTANCE
4.5–6.4 km return

ELEVATION GAIN
112 m

DIFFICULTY
Moderate, recommended for children aged 5 and older. Good signed trail throughout. Note there are lots of ups and downs throughout that may take a toll on young legs.

SEASON
Late spring, summer and fall.

OF SPECIAL INTEREST FOR CHILDREN
Terrific lake scenery and a few opportunities to dip your feet (or more!) in the crystal clear waters. Dogs are not allowed on this trail.

1. The trail is well signed and very easy to follow. Hike 1.1 km to a signed junction and follow the signs to First Lake.

2. Reaching First Lake, it's worth it to follow faint trails to the shoreline for a few minutes to get additional views of this beautiful lake.

3. Return to the main trail and hike to the remaining lakes, enjoying the stunning array of colours. Note that the Second

Lake is prone to very low water levels. The land bridge between the Third and Fourth lakes is a great place to take a break and then explore a little.

4. There is an unofficial trail circling the Fifth Lake (1.9 km in length), but most choose to forgo this side trip and simply follow the loop, eventually arriving back at the signed junction. From there, return the same way you came in.

CKWISE FROM TOP Looking back on the stunning Third Lake; The pier of the Fifth Lake is a terrific t for photos and relaxation; Hubert, Amélie with Amandine, and Olivia, from Quebec City, oying the Fourth Lake.

42. PATH OF THE GLACIER/CAVELL MEADOWS

In one word: awesome!

LOCATION
From Jasper, drive 6.7 km south on Highway 93 and turn right onto Highway 93A (towards Mount Edith Cavell Road). Follow the narrow, winding road for about 14 km to its end. If arriving from the south, the turnoff is 2 km north of the turnoff to the Valley of the Five Lakes.

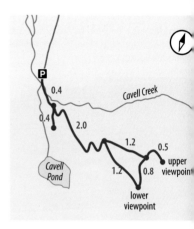

DISTANCE
8.3 km for all trails

ELEVATION GAIN
377 m; high point: 2288 m

DIFFICULTY
Strenuous, recommended for children aged 7 and older (younger children could complete the Path of the Glacier and the lower viewpoint). Good trail throughout, with several steep sections of rocky terrain.

SEASON
Summer and early fall.

OF SPECIAL INTEREST FOR CHILDREN
Close-up view of a hanging glacier and the colourful pond its meltwater creates. Dogs are not allowed on this trail.

1. Due to the excellent signage throughout, a specific route description is unnecessary. Instead, a few helpful hints are offered:
    - Complete the Path of the Glacier trail first, to a great view of Cavell Pond and Angel Glacier. Do *not* ignore the warnings about going past the barrier to get to the pond. In 2012 a huge chunk of the adjacent glacier (Ghost Glacier) calved off into the pond. The resulting wave

The hike starts with a great view of Mount Edith Cavell's famed East Ridge ourtesy Shawn Benbow); Jennifer and Shawn Benbow and the best view of the day from the lower wpoint (Courtesy Shawn Benbow); Cavell Pond is an exquisite hue of milky turquoise (Courtesy awn Benbow).

of water decimated everything in its path, including a portion of the parking lot (which has now been relocated at a safer distance).

- For Cavell Meadows, the lower viewpoint (2118 m) offers the best view of Cavell Pond and Mount Sorrow above it (simply an outlier of Mount Edith Cavell).

- The higher viewpoint (2288 m) offers the best view of Mount Edith Cavell. This route is quite steep and a little loose in places.

43. OLD FORT POINT LOOP

If you and the family are looking for a great view of the Jasper area (with minimal effort) this route will do the trick.

LOCATION
From downtown Jasper, follow Highway 93A (Hazel Avenue) for 1 km southeast, and turn left onto Old Fort Point/Lac Beauvert Road. Follow this road for 1 km, over the Athabasca River, and turn right, into the Old Fort Point parking lot.

DISTANCE
3.7–4.2-km loop

ELEVATION GAIN
130 m; high point: 1170 m

DIFFICULTY
Moderate, recommended for children aged 5 and older. Good trail throughout, with some steep sections on descent.

SEASON
Spring, summer and fall.

OF SPECIAL INTEREST FOR CHILDREN
The kids will love the rocky summit and the view. Do the loop in a clockwise direction so everyone gets their exercise before the pleasant summit surprise. If time and energy are limited, go counterclockwise to the summit, then return the same way you came in. Dogs are not allowed on this trail.

1.   Note the wooden staircase to the left of the trailhead kiosk – that is where you will be returning from. From the trailhead kiosk, follow the number 1 route all the way.

2. At the 1.5-km mark the trail forks. Both forks work and end up at the same place. The right fork is 0.5 km, while the left is 1.0 km and less steep. Take your pick.

3. When the trails join together, continue following the number 1 route, now heading back in the general direction of the parking lot. A couple of red Adirondack chairs provide a quick and scenic diversion along the way. The summit is an interesting rocky plateau, with open views in every direction. Spend some time here, letting the kids explore, and then continue following the trail down the other side. This section is steep and extra care is warranted. Finish the trip with great views of the Athabasca River and a staircase descent.

OCKWISE FROM LEFT The Adirondack chairs also provide a great view of the famed mountain ourtesy Brigid Meegan Scott); From the summit, a stunning sunset over Pyramid Mountain ourtesy Brigid Meegan Scott); Noah Koob ascends the steep descent route, made easier by steps rved into the rock (Courtesy Tanya Koob).

44. LAKE ANNETTE

Easy, scenic and ideal for families.

LOCATION
From downtown Jasper, drive north and turn onto Highway 16. Follow the signs to Maligne Lake. Once on the other side of the Athabasca River, turn right, following the signs to Lake Annette. There are many places to park that give easy access to the lake.

DISTANCE
2.4-km loop

ELEVATION GAIN
Minimal

DIFFICULTY
Very easy, recommended for all. Excellent paved and wheelchair-accessible trail around the lake.

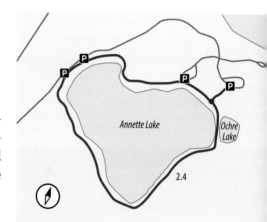

SEASON
Spring, summer and fall.

OF SPECIAL INTEREST FOR CHILDREN
Go for a swim, boat on the lake, play in the playground, but don't forget to hike around the lake! The trail is stroller-friendly. Dogs are not allowed on this trail.

1. From any of the multiple parking areas, find the paved trail and hike around the lake in either direction. The east side is peaceful and serene, while the north and west sides usually have more activity. There is a small beach for swimming, a pier for boat activities and a playground.

FACING PAGE FROM TOP James, Shawn, Walter and Jennifer Benbow get ready for the hike (Courtesy Shawn Benbow); Looking across Lake Annette from the southeast shore (Courtesy Shawn Benbow); James Benbow has found something of interest along the paved trail (Courtesy Shawn Benbow).

45. MALIGNE CANYON

One of the premier canyons in the Canadian Rockies.
Not to be missed if you are in the area.

LOCATION
From downtown Jasper, drive north and turn onto Highway 16 and follow the signs to Maligne Lake. Once on the other side of the Athabasca River, turn left, drive 6 km and turn left again into the Maligne Canyon parking lot.

DISTANCE
1–4.4 km

ELEVATION LOSS/ GAIN
50–100 m

DIFFICULTY
Easy to moderate (depending how far down you go), recommended for children aged 4 and older. Excellent trail throughout.

SEASON
Late spring, summer and early fall.

OF SPECIAL INTEREST FOR CHILDREN
Observe the power of water in the form of this stunning canyon. Dogs are not allowed on this trail.

1. No description is necessary, as the trails are well signed and easy to follow. The recommendation for families is to descend a little ways past the Fourth Bridge and then return the same way, but on the opposite side of the canyon for a little variety. Fences protect from a fall into the canyon very well, but obviously you'll still want to keep an eye on the little ones. If you have two vehicles available, leave one in the Fifth Bridge parking lot and hike down to it.

FROM TOP A good opportunity to talk to the kids about the power of water erosion; The bridges offer awesome views down the canyon (Courtesy Shawn Benbow); The picturesque Fifth Bridge (Courtesy Shawn Benbow).

46. OPAL HILLS

*A steep forest hike to a wonderful valley
and viewpoint high above Maligne Lake.*

LOCATION
From downtown Jasper, drive north and turn onto Highway 16 and follow the signs to Maligne Lake. Once on the other side of the Athabasca River, turn left and drive 50 km to the lake. Upon reaching the Maligne Lake area, turn left into the first parking lot, then left again and uphill to reach the farthest of the three lots. The trail begins at the northeast corner.

DISTANCE
8.2-km loop

ELEVATION GAIN
500 m; high point: 2250 m

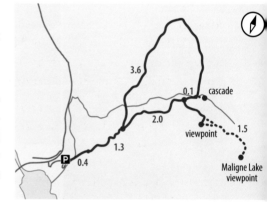

DIFFICULTY
Very strenuous, recommended for children aged 10 and older. Good but steep trail for much of the ascent.

SEASON
Summer and early fall.

OF SPECIAL INTEREST FOR CHILDREN
A quieter alternative to Bald Hills but equally strenuous. Older kids will appreciate this one. Dogs are not allowed on this trail.

1. You will be following the number 22 trail all the way. From the trailhead, hike a few hundred metres to a signed junction and take the left fork.

2. About 1.3 km of initially easy, but then relentlessly steep, hiking takes you to the next junction.

3. Take the left fork. It is longer but less steep and far more scenic. Save the other route for descent. Follow the left fork up into the valley. The trail then wraps around two hills. The big peak above you to the east is Opal Peak (a good scramble for when the kids are no longer kids). This section of the trail is 3.6 km long and eventually crosses a stream.

4. After crossing the stream you will arrive at a T-junction. Going left here takes you to a small cascade in a few hundred metres. Return to the junction if you choose this minor diversion. Going right is the continuation of trail 22.

5. Quickly you will arrive at a four-way junction. Going right here is the continuation of 22 and this is the route you will descend. However, going left and up is almost mandatory

CKWISE FROM TOP LEFT A hiker breaks out into the scenic upper valley (Courtesy Explorejasper.com); e highlight of the trip for most will be this view of Maligne Lake (Courtesy Explorejasper.com); ppy hikers celebrate their achievement (Courtesy Explorejasper.com).

FROM TOP View from the Maligne viewpoint – not bad even in miserable weather; Gaining elevation towards Maligne Lake Viewpoint – over the ridge, to the right; Snow patches can make for an exhilarating descent (Courtesy Explorejasper.com).

at this point. Even if you don't complete the Going Farther extension, it's only a short, steep hike to a wonderful view of Maligne Lake. Hike up the trail until it forks. Take the right fork and within 20 seconds you will be rewarded with that view.

6. Return to the four-way junction and hike down 22, eventually reaching the junction mentioned in point 3 above. Return the same way you came in from there.

Going Farther: Maligne Lake Viewpoint
Stunning views of the lake and surrounding mountains.

Distance
Add 3 km return

Elevation Gain
Add 280 m; high point: 2430 m

Difficulty
Very strenuous, recommended for children aged 12 and older. Good trail to start with and then faint to no trails to the summit.

1. From the four-way junction, follow the steep trail up, going east. Take either fork higher up and continue up the wide ridge.

2. The trail soon fades away. Continue going up the stable scree but trend more to the right.

3. Eventually you will see Maligne Lake Viewpoint. It is not the highest point of the ridge but an obvious grassy knoll. Make your way over there and take in the wonderful view. Return the same way you came in.

47. BALD HILLS

Little legs will get a great workout to perhaps the best view of Maligne Lake in the area.

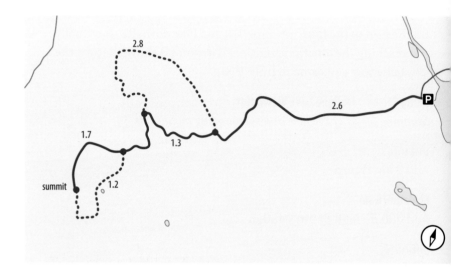

LOCATION
From downtown Jasper, drive north and turn onto Highway 16 and follow the signs to Maligne Lake. Once on the other side of the Athabasca River, turn left and drive 50 km to the lake. Upon reaching the Maligne Lake area, drive past the lake outlet and follow the signs to the Bald Hills/Skyline parking lot.

DISTANCE
13.2 km return

ELEVATION GAIN
567 m; high point: 2320 m

DIFFICULTY
Very strenuous, recommended for children aged 12 and older. Easy fire road, followed by a steep grind up a trail with lots of tree roots, then a good trail to the summit.

From near the site of the old lookout, the false summit of the objective can be seen. Note the barely visible trail going up the left side – aim for it (Courtesy Shawn Benbow).

SEASON
Summer and early fall.

OF SPECIAL INTEREST FOR CHILDREN
Pick a clear day so an amazing summit view will be the reward for the kids' aching legs. Dogs are not allowed on this trail.

1. From the parking lot, cross the road and find the trailhead kiosk. Hike up the fire road for about 2.6 km.

2. At the 2.6-km mark, look for a trail on the left side of the fire road. Turn left onto that trail and follow it steeply upward for 1.3 km. (Note: You can also stay on the fire road, but this adds 1.5 km one-way to the trip).

3. At the T-junction at the top of the steep trail, turn left. The right fork goes to an open area where an old fire lookout used to be – a good place for a quick rest if the kids (or adults) need one.

4. Hike this trail for a few hundred metres, arriving at another junction. Both routes go to the summit. The left fork goes there more directly and is the one described here.

Jennifer Benbow hikes the obvious route to the summit from the false summit (Courtesy Shawn Benbow).

5. Hike this new trail and watch for a steep, rocky trail that branches off to the right and winds its way up to the top. Take this trail.

6. At the top, continue on the obvious trail to the interesting summit of Bald Hills. On a clear day the view will amaze you.

7. For the super-adventurous family, there are options to continue exploring the area to the south. Most people will choose to return the same way they came in. For some added variety on the initial part of the return trip, you can descend the south ridge until a minor trail on your left takes you back to a main trail. The return route is obvious after that.

FACING PAGE, CLOCKWISE FROM TOP The premier view of the day: a close-up of Samson Peak and Maligne Lake (Courtesy Shawn Benbow); Hikers returning from some exploration of the high points to the south. Note all the well-trodden trails (Courtesy Brigid Meegan Scott); A more comprehensive view from the summit (Courtesy Shawn Benbow); The Benbows enjoying one of the best summits in the area (Courtesy Shawn Benbow).

IMPORTANT CONTACTS

Kananaskis Country Trail Reports
1.877.537.2757
www.albertaparks.ca/parks/kananaskis/kananaskis-country/
advisories-public-safety/trail-reports/

Barrier Lake Information Centre
7 km south of Highway 1 on Highway 40
403.678.0760
www.albertaparks.ca/parks/kananaskis/bow-val-
ley-pp/information-facilities/kananaskis-contacts/
barrier-lake-visitor-information-centre/

Peter Lougheed Park Discovery & Information Centre
Kananaskis Trail
403.678.0760
www.albertaparks.ca/parks/kananaskis/peter-
lougheed-pp/information-facilities/kananaskis-contacts/
peter-lougheed-park-discovery-information-centre/

Banff National Park Information Centre
224 Banff Avenue, Banff
403.762.1550
www.pc.gc.ca/eng/pn-np/ab/banff

Lake Louise Visitor Centre
201 Village Rd., next to Samson Mall, Lake Louise
403.522.3833
www.pc.gc.ca/eng/pn-np/ab/banff/visit.aspx

Yoho Visitor Centre
Field, BC
250.343.6783
www.pc.gc.ca/en/pn-np/bc/yoho

The Nugara kids and mum head down to the Elbow River from the Paddy's Flat trail.

Jasper Visitor Centre
500 Connaught Drive, Jasper
780.852.6176
Trails Office: 780-852-6177
www.pc.gc.ca/en/pn-np/ab/jasper/visit/heures-hours

Emergency
Dial 911

Excellent scenery en route to Helen Lake.

ACKNOWLEDGEMENTS

Once again a huge thank you to Tanya Koob, for photos, invaluable information and inspiration. Thank you to Gillean and Tony Daffern for paving the way for so many of us in the Canadian Rockies. Also to Lynda Pianosi and Brenda Kurtz Lenko for authoring their family hiking guidebooks. And thank you to the following individuals for their photo contributions: Jennifer Benbow, Shawn Benbow, Connie Biggart, Par Boora, Matthew Clay, Chris Doering, Mark Fioretti, Gordon Hobbs, Matthew Hobbs, Greg Jones, Stacey Jones, Melissa Kindt, Denise Kitagawa and family, Mark Koob, Nicole Lisafeld, Leigh McAdam, Mark Nugara, Brigid Meegan Scott, Christian Skogen, Amélie Stavric, Marko Stavric, Karen Ung, Kheang Ung, Amy Wong and Eddie Wong.

DISCLAIMER

There are inherent risks in hiking mountain areas that require hikers to constantly use their own judgment. Anyone using this book does so at their own risk, and both the author and the publisher disclaim any liability for any injuries or other damage that may be sustained by anyone hiking any of the trails described in this book.

Be aware that bear sightings and fire hazard can close trails at a moment's notice. Flash floods can wash out bridges. Fallen trees resulting from strong winds can block trails and make the going difficult.

In this book there are no dos and don'ts. It is assumed that users are caring, intelligent people who will respect the country they are travelling through and its wildlife.

OVE Pretty sweet views of Snowdome and Mount Kitchener early on during the Wilcox Pass
ke. **FOLLOWING SPREAD** The sublime environs of Arethusa Cirque.

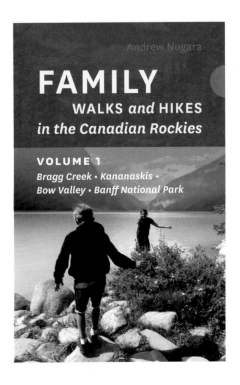

Family Walks and Hikes in the Canadian Rockies

– Volume 1

Bragg Creek - Kananaskis - Bow Valley - Banff National Park

BY ANDREW NUGARA

9781771602242

The first book for the Canadian Rockies in the series brings together an inspiring collection of comfortable walks and spectacular hikes for visitors and locals looking for unique, guided wanderings in a number of diverse locations in the Rockies.

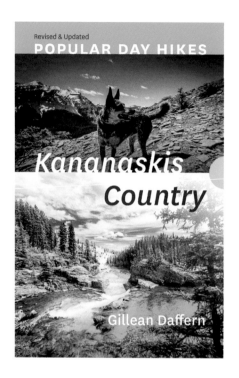

Popular Day Hikes:
Kananaskis Country

– Revised & Updated

BY GILLEAN DAFFERN

9781771602655

Kananaskis Country is located on the eastern slopes of
the Canadian Rockies and includes the areas of Canmore,
Bow Valley, Peter Lougheed Provincial Park, Highwood,
Elbow, Kananaskis Valley, Smith-Dorrien, Sheep and
Jumpingpound. From easy, short day walks to ridgewalks
there is something in this volume for everyone.

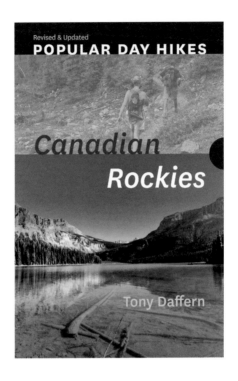

Popular Day Hikes:
Canadian Rockies

— Revised & Updated

BY TONY DAFFERN

9781771602679

Covering accessible trails in one of the world's most
stunningly beautiful natural environments, this colourful
guide features easy short-day walks, more-strenuous full-
day hikes and the occasional easy scramble around Banff,
Lake Louise and Moraine Lake, the Icefields Parkway,
Kootenay National Park, Yoho National Park and Jasper.